CONCEALED CARRY

CONCEALED CARRY

The Shooter's Guide to Selecting Handguns

WILEY CLAPP

PALADIN PRESS · BOULDER, COLORADO

Contents

Preface

**W**hen the idea for this book was in the discussion stages, the late Colonel Rex Applegate agreed to write a foreword to it. Before we went to press, Col. Applegate passed away; there are no introductory remarks by this legendary warrior patriot. In my view, no one else could possibly fill his shoes in this or any other effort and the book will have to suffice as I have written it. While I am fairly pleased with the book and considered dedicating it to his memory, I have to accept that this slim volume is hardly worthy of mention in the same breath as the life of Colonel Rex Applegate.

So I ask only that you remember him. If the men of the World War II era were indeed the greatest generation, he was clearly the best of them.

—Wiley Clapp
Minden, Nevada
October 2000

The Need for Concealed-Carry Handguns

Americans carry handguns. Most of the time, it's completely legal because a particular handgunner happens to live where the required license is obtainable. Some of the major Eastern cities and states are notoriously unwilling to license folks for defensive concealed carry, but the pressure continues for those places to wake up and smell the coffee.

If you live in a jurisdiction that has "shall issue" provisions, you're in good shape. If you don't, you have no recourse but to get involved in the political process and change the law. Such a hotly contested issue must have its origins in some real need; look at your daily newspaper and the need for the law-abiding to carry guns leaps right out at you. Plainly stated, the criminals are carrying guns in complete violation of the law and they don't care. I do not imply that you should also violate the law. Rather, I would prefer to see you go through the all-important training, get your license, and select a proper handgun with which to defend yourself. The process of selection is what this book is all about.

In my opinion, the right to carry a gun lies in the explicit wording of the Second Amendment. Constitutional scholars continue to debate what the framers of the grand old document really meant when they composed that single sentence,

"A well-regulated militia being necessary to the security of a free state, the right of the people to keep and bear arms shall not be infringed."

Is that hard to understand? It isn't for me, but men more intelligent than I have succeeded in muddling things to the point that many now believe we don't need guns. And to be out front about it, I am not talking about sporting weapons for recreational use; I am talking about plain fighting or combat handguns, the ones you habitually carry on your person. They're there to resolve violent criminal attacks on you and yours that seem to be more common

Americans carry guns. Headed off to work, this young man has a powerful pistol concealed on his person. He also has considerable training in its use.

Americans carry guns. As she heads out the front door to go jogging, she has a small revolver in her waist pack, along with the concealed-carry license.

now than they were in the frontier period before some people "interpreted" the Constitution for their own ends.

I take no particular joy in the fact that there's a need for honest citizens to go armed and loaded, but the need is very strong. There is a great deal of violence in the streets and it has sometimes made its way to living rooms via home invasions. I moved to my present home, a super little cattle-ranching community in Nevada, to get away from the urban nightmare that is the Los Angeles basin. Sure, there's much less street crime, but still we've had the peace and dignity of the community upset by shooting incidents that peace officers have had

to risk their necks to resolve. Anywhere you care to mention, there is some form of violent criminal behavior that potentially threatens the lives of innocent people. If you are reading this book, I am probably preaching to the choir. The point is simply that there's enough violence to justify the decisions of anyone who chooses to get a good license, better training, and the best gun he can possibly find.

But I would also counsel those who agree with this reasoning to go through the procedure for licensing even if they prefer not to go habitually armed. The logic of that is self-serving to a degree, because I want as many citizens as

What could possibly be clearer? The Founding Fathers intended that we have guns—and the right to carry them—when they wrote the famous words into the Constitution.

possible to use the rights given them by the lawmakers. If you accept the need for concealed-carry weapon (CCW) permits and don't get one, then the statistics will show one less valid permit in force. Eventually, some bureaucratic bean counter will count noses and solemnly advise the legislature that the CCW permit couldn't be that important because only 2.2 percent of the population has applied for them. If nothing else, you help perpetuate the rights of others to carry, even when you don't wish to exercise the same right for yourself.

A handgun on your person changes a lot of things about the way you lead your life. Accept

that a gun can be misused rather dramatically. You cannot allow your normal good judgement to be affected by rage in situations that might fully justify plenty of anger but not deadly force. The one that comes quickly to mind is driving on the nation's streets and highways. If someone outrageously cuts you off and completes the insult with the screaming, honking, and gesturing we've all seen, it means he or she is a rude, impolite, and even a dangerous driver. This is not grounds for summary execution; the gun you're carrying stays out of sight. In similar fashion, you can't be in public places with a concealed handgun and a snootful of 96-proof Old Popskull or any other legal or illegal substance that materially changes your perceptions and adversely influences your judgement.

Accepting the right to carry a defensive firearm consequently involves also accepting the need to behave like a gentleman (or lady) when one of life's stressful encounters comes along. Guns belong in purses, pockets, or holsters until the clear and present danger of death or serious injury presents itself. Only then is it time to fight.

I have run this next logic past a couple of different judges: The court system will probably find your shooting a human being justified if it can be shown that you were in real fear of your life and had no other options. If it looks like you were shooting to punish illegal or impolite behavior, you have a problem. Hard-nosed right wingers might argue this is all wrong, but I don't think so. To me it's relatively simple and the more I write about handguns and their use, the more certain I am that shooting is a last resort.

You also need to understand what your introduction of that little .38 will likely do to a confrontation in progress. TV has conditioned us to believe that drawing a gun on a person and commanding manfully *"Freeze!"* will bring the proceedings to an immediate halt. Don't bet on it, pardner. I have seen a number of these incidents have exactly the opposite effect. Instead of slowing down the action, presenting the gun accelerates things. The same is true of warning shots. I know of a case where an off-duty policeman almost went to prison because he fired a warning shot at the ground in front of a mob of drunks. Some drunken fool in the back of the group yelled "It was a blank!" and our hero watched the mob advance with busted pool cues in their hands. He fired once again with life-altering results because the drunk he shot and killed simply didn't see the gun as a threat and continued his homicidal advance. Guns are not magic wands that make all evil go away; they're deadly weapons.

Another point that needs a minute or two: ask yourself if you can really shoot if the need arises. I attended a class once where a good instructor struggled with a woman who was sent to the class by her husband. She was so tearfully terrified by the prospect of violence, even in her own defense, that she had trouble even touching the gun, much less using it with any resolve at all. This doesn't mean she's a wimp, but rather a person with an

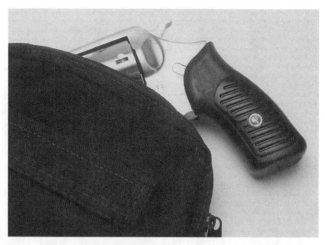

Leave the gun in the pack until the need to use it is obvious. Brandishing a gun without justification is a crime in most jurisdictions.

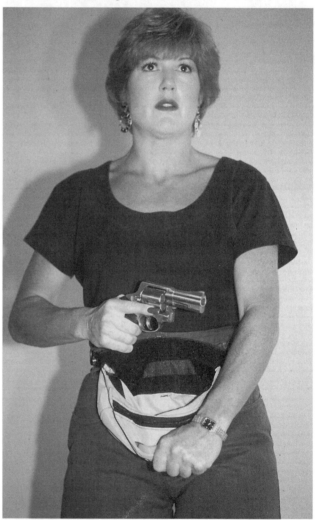

Drawing a gun when threatened may stop the unprovoked attack. But then again, maybe it won't. Be prepared to shoot in the face of a deadly threat.

Whatever gun you choose, train with it regularly. The Colt Commander is a fine firearm, but you need to practice with it often to use it skillfully under pressure.

arguably exaggerated regard for the sanctity of human life. In conversations with her after the class, I learned that she had been traumatized by several unfortunate incidents in her childhood. The lady was a gentle soul who was possibly the world's worst candidate for a CCW permit. Her attitude was rather passive and far short of the mindset of John Holliday and the Earp brothers as they strode down that dusty street in Tombstone.

If someone's moral, ethical, or religious convictions are such that taking another human being's life is out of the question, guns are just not for them; preparations for trouble should involve good locks and better tactics, possibly even a first-rate pair of running shoes.

But if the implement you use for personal defense is, by design, a deadly weapon, the effectiveness of one over another becomes a question of what stops the fight quickest. It is an inexact science and that's for sure. Your shooting

your gun must be defensive and intended to stop the fight or halt the attack, not to kill. It's paradoxical, but the gun-ammo combination that best serves to stop the fight might also be at least among the best in its likelihood of killing. We have had a great deal of progress with regards to handgun and ammunition effectiveness in the past few years, but we have yet to find a way to shoot somebody and not have the possibility of his demise.

As one who spent a goodly portion of his adult life working as a peace officer, I can attest to the fact that the thin blue line of police protection is indeed very thin. There are only as many good coppers on the streets as the carefully kept statistics tell us are needed for a reasonable degree of crime suppression. As a practical matter, the number of units fielded always falls short of what is needed, mostly because of budget constraints. This is the basis for the cliché about the presence

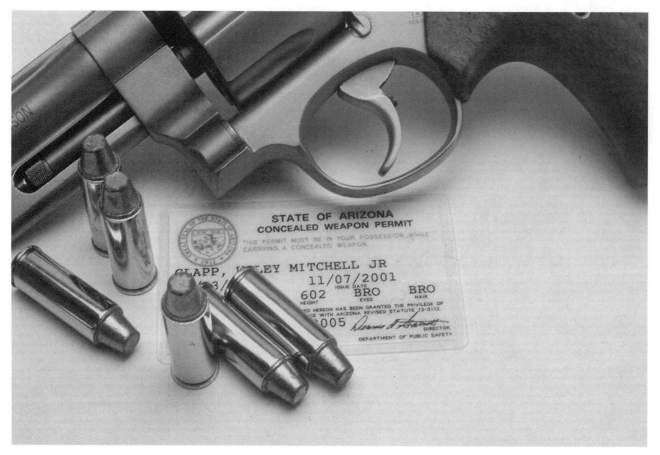

If your local laws require it, obtain and carry a concealed-carry weapon permit whenever you are armed. Violate no law in regards to carrying your gun. Avoid a fight whenever possible.

of policemen and need for policeman—an inverse ratio. Sure, call for John Law if you possibly can, but accept the fact that close immediate defense away from your home is up to you. Just like it always has been.

Before we leave the subject of constitutional rights and practical matters, we'd do well to reflect for a moment on the words of philosopher/author/patriot Robert A. Heinlein. One of his many pithy little quotes seems particularly apropos in this regard: "*An armed society is a polite society.*" Once we were a scrupulously polite, but still gentle nation of tough-minded, self-reliant frontiersmen who left the Old World to escape the tyranny that kept us, among other things, from owning and bearing arms. We managed our own lives and safety. In many ways, things have changed. But although much has changed, I cling to the belief that most Americans still have the courage to defend themselves. I also believe that the more they are allowed to do so, the less there'll be a need to do so. This book is simply a careful dissertation on the means of getting it done.

Choosing the Right Gun

CHAPTER

2

he question is deceptively simple: "What is the best handgun to use when you are suddenly attacked out on the street?" The answer is both simplistic and prophetic: "...the gun you have with you." As the gunwriter's cliché holds, the first rule of winning a gunfight is to have a gun. If you don't carry one, you must be prepared for the consequences of an armed attack (good luck). The answer to the original question is one of those utterly obvious ones like why did the chicken cross the road. It's the implications of the answer that makes for a chapter in this book.

Even before we get into models and calibers, inches and ounces, we have to understand the complexity of the selection process and how so many people end up with the wrong gun. Assuming you asked me "Wiley, what is the best handgun to carry for the possibility of being attacked?" I might unhesitatingly respond "A high-capacity .45 auto." That is true and I have several of them. But human nature remains unchanged and I (and most other defensive handgunners) am not comfortable with a pistol of that size. I therefore compromise and carry something smaller and lighter, but still adequately powerful to get the job done.

If you are in a similar situation and choose a particular handgun, either pistol or revolver, only to find that the gun is heavy, bulky, and awkward to carry, you won't carry it. You will avoid the discomfort and go unarmed. Let's hope that it doesn't happen on the day that trouble comes.

No thinking person would want to routinely carry a handgun on his person unless he was convinced there was a need to do so. Murphy monitors this situation closely and you can bet the longer you go without your gun, the sooner the day comes when you need it and don't have it. Even the lightest handguns make awkward lumps in your pocket. Scores of gun-savvy holster designers give it

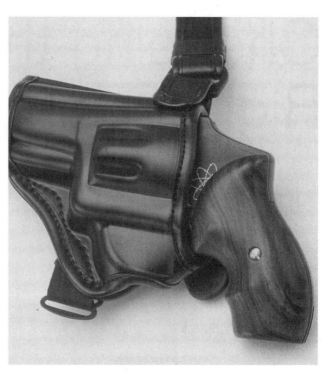

What's the best possible gun to carry against the possibility of attack? It's an imponderable question, but this high-capacity Glock meets many of the important criteria. It's fairly light and compact, has a good capacity, and it's chambered for a powerful round.

Choose something that is easy to carry. That means a light gun above all else. The rounded corners of this light S&W Centennial make it very easy to carry under any kind of clothing.

Recent advances in metallurgy permit S&W to offer a 12-ounce .357 Magnum. It kicks like a mule, but it carries like a hummingbird. A simple DAO firearm.

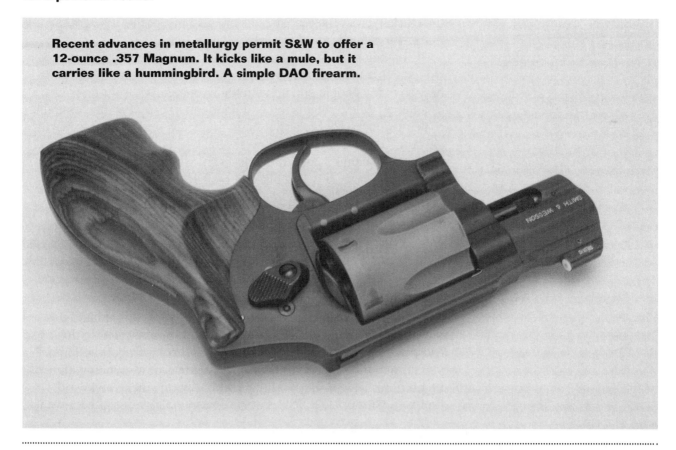

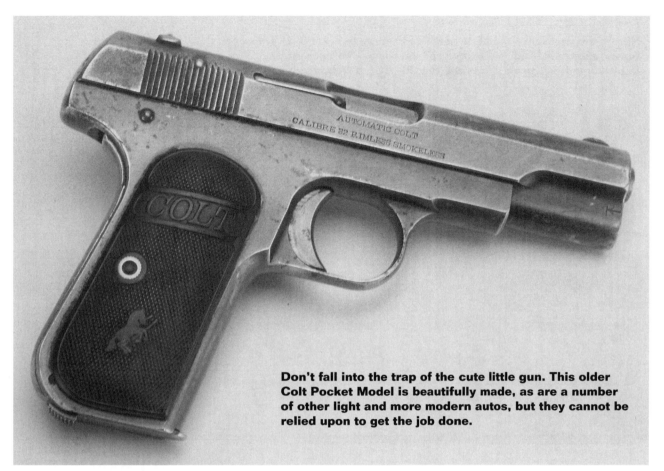

Don't fall into the trap of the cute little gun. This older Colt Pocket Model is beautifully made, as are a number of other light and more modern autos, but they cannot be relied upon to get the job done.

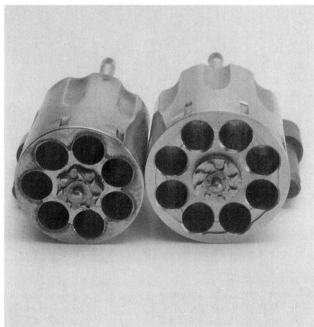

Even revolver makers have been caught up in the capacity race. These are the cylinders from newly introduced guns that started out as six-guns—the S&W L-frame seven-shot and N-frame eight-shot.

their best shot and come away with ingenious holsters to ease the CCW permit holder's burden, but there's still a certain amount of weight and bulk to a defensive handgun; only rarely does the gun and carrying system get to the point where you just don't notice the gun. I won't tell you how (yet), but I have personally settled on a gun and holster combination that is so compatible with my lifestyle that I really don't know the gun is there. Presumably, I will remember when the time comes.

I don't want to belabor the point, but this matter is extremely important. It's the search for a perfect gun—accurate, shootable, and powerful, but reduced in visibility and weight so as to be your constant companion. It's one thing to carry a high-capacity automatic pistol in the winter when you wear long, heavy coats and parkas, but quite another matter in the summer when you vacation in Balboa and wear shorts or swimming trunks all the time. There are several factors that go into making an informed choice. Let's take a quick look at them.

Here's the problem—the slide markings tell us the gun is chambered for an outmoded and underpowered cartridge. No amount of improvement in ammo will make the .32 ACP a fighting cartridge.

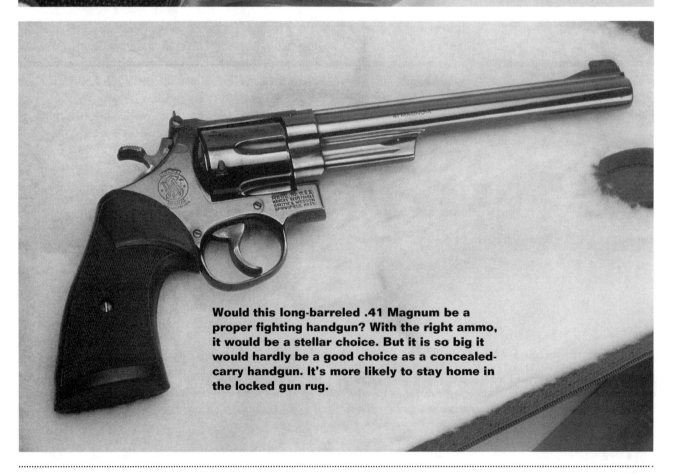

Would this long-barreled .41 Magnum be a proper fighting handgun? With the right ammo, it would be a stellar choice. But it is so big it would hardly be a good choice as a concealed-carry handgun. It's more likely to stay home in the locked gun rug.

Your chosen armament needs to be sufficiently powerful to get the job done when called upon to do so. This rules out some mightily attractive little pistols and revolvers, simply because their ammunition characteristics don't hold up under field use. Yeah, I know: "It's better than nothin'." But why should you carry a handgun that all reasonable evidence tells you won't reliably stop fights? What are you carrying for? To *lose* the first and probably only fight which you're ever likely to see? Robert Ruark's book title sends a powerful message—*Use Enough Gun.*

The deeper you dig into this business of what constitutes *enough* gun, the more complex the questions become. Obviously, we'll be trying to compromise between the gun's size and weight, opposed to its capacity and caliber. But the more we compromise, the more it becomes obvious a lighter, smaller, easier-to-carry pistol must also be one that is capable of decisive effect. You give up something when you take another ounce off the gun or another round out of its cylinder or magazine. What's left had better be capable of getting it done. As we approach the new century

in a fundamentally gun-hostile society, it is nothing short of astounding how much variety the gunmakers offer. You can literally have it your way as you go about the selection process.

Standing at the gun store counter, the shooter faces some weighty (no pun intended) decisions about how much gun he's going to buy and hide on his person. If he chooses something too heavy, then quickly begins the rationalization process that leaves the handgun safely locked away in a nice suede gun rug on the top shelf of the hall closet—*at home*—he has made a poor choice. For this reason, I place a very high priority on light weight. Human nature being what it is, we all naturally seek to avoid discomfort, so I believe we need to face reality and pick something that will be there when we need it. As long as it is adequate for personal defense, the lighter gun is probably the better gun for discrete carry. Don't worry, we are going to spend a lot of time dealing with "adequate" in the next couple of chapters.

The size of the gun is closely related to its weight. We are in the midst of a revolution of sorts when it comes to building ever-smaller guns, but

Here's a pair of .45 autos. The big Para-Ordnance holds 13+1 rounds, while the little Kimber is a 6+1. How much capacity will you sacrifice to get a gun that you carry all the time? It's not a brand choice, either—Kimber makes big ones, Para makes small ones.

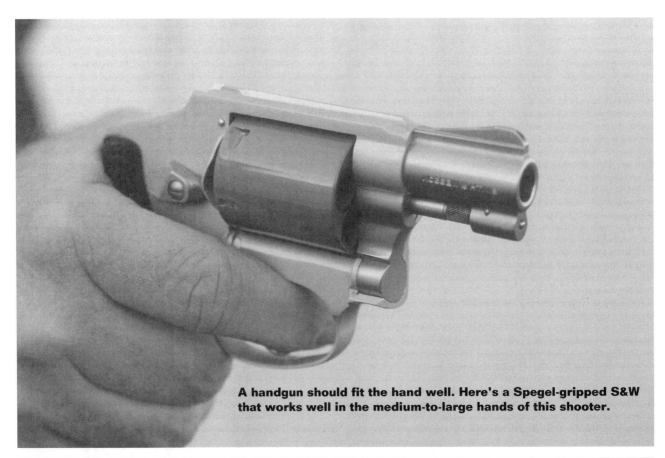

A handgun should fit the hand well. Here's a Spegel-gripped S&W that works well in the medium-to-large hands of this shooter.

The Glock Model 17 has the greatest capacity of any commonly seen service pistol at 17+1. There's a great deal to commend the pistol, but its capacity is pretty far down the list. Beyond a point, having more rounds on tap offers diminishing returns.

The shape of the handgun impacts its ability to be concealed. This shooter has a small revolver in his trousers pocket and you would probably never realize it.

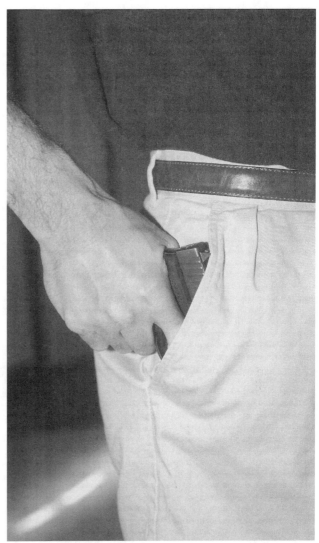

The squared contours of a small auto are a little harder to conceal than those of a revolver when they are both carried in pockets. The same is generally true when they are carried in most types of holsters.

we are even deeper into building ever-lighter guns. Obviously, if it's bigger, it's almost certainly going to be heavier. The point is simply that you can get a pretty decent-sized pistol that is surprisingly light. That's great, but at this juncture, another nagging little difficulty crops up.

A big pistol or revolver is harder to hide than a little one. Worse yet, it's likely to be harder to deploy. In an emergency, deploying the pistol is something that has a certain immediacy about it. If we should be so unfortunate as to come under criminal attack at a time and place where withdrawal from the scene is not an option, then

we're going to want to get done what needs to be done right damned now. A large pistol in a deep parka pocket, sacklike purse, or snug fanny pack can sometimes be hard to manage quickly. Therefore a pistol of more reasonable size might be a better choice when it comes to speedy deployment.

The shape of a gun sometimes affects the speed with which it may be drawn from concealment. Unless they are treated to some extensive custom gunsmithing, many handguns have too many edges, corners, and projections for rapid use. Depending on the nature of the gun, only so much modifying can be done. Fortunately,

Once you decide on a handgun type, you can choose from several sizes. These three revolvers are all S&W .357 Magnums, but they are built on three different frames and have five-, six- and seven-shot cylinders.

several makers have focused on this problem and have done a lot to resolve this handgunner's dilemma. Guns like Glocks, Kahrs, Sigmas, and Steyrs are deliberately contrived to have minimal controls and all of those are as non-interfering as possible. They are shaped to be carried easily and drawn swiftly.

You also have to realize that the shape of a handgun impacts that firearm's ability to be concealed. There is a great deal that goes into resolving this problem, but the effect of not resolving it is a firearm that "prints" through your clothing and announces to the world that you are "packin' iron." Many authors have waxed eloquent on the ability of a flat little automatic to just slip away and hide. But when you really try it, a small revolver often conceals better than a small auto. Although it may be somewhat thick through the middle where the cylinder is located, the little revolver has very irregular contours. Most often, the shape of an auto is two straight lines (formed

by the butt and the slide/barrel unit) which meet at a slight angle. That regular junction sticks out like a sore thumb. Properly fitted holsters and carefully selected clothing can help a lot in concealing your shooter. Indeed, if you opt for a bigger gun, proper holsters and clothing are essential.

And if all these considerations were not enough, a person's hand size and physical stature impact their choice of a hideout handgun. Hand size is particularly important in a woman's choice of a defensive handgun. Obviously, females tend to have smaller hands to match their generally smaller stature. In teaching shooters of both genders, I have concluded that the only real difference is the size of the hand. It is therefore essential that women shooters choose and use guns they are really capable of handling. There's nothing patronizing about this; many women are capable of handling pistols the size of Colt .45 automatics. But shooters of either sex need guns they can manage and it is a definite factor in gun selection.

Even height and body confirmation bear on the choice of a defensive firearm. Consider the situation of my friend Geoff Keogh, who is a well-proportioned young man standing over 6-foot, 4-inches tall. There's so much distance between Geoff's beltline and his armpit that he could easily wear an underarm holster holding an 8 3/8-inch barreled S&W .44 Magnum or even a Desert Eagle auto in .50 AE. Both are guns at the extreme end of the size spectrum and probably never going to be used as concealed-carry firearms, but Geoff *could* do it if he chose. Now look at Geoff's petite wife, Liz. She's about 5-foot, 1-inch and could neither carry nor conceal such monstrous firearms. Trying to carry a gun that's way out of your size range should be an obvious no-no. I make the point only in the hopes that you will make this an element on your shopping checklist and avoid guns that are even just a little out of the size range. When they are in that category, the rationalization will begin.

There is one other point that we need to address here because so many shooters get hung up on it when they are buying, particularly for the first time. In recent years, the makers got into a real war about the capacity of their pistols. It got to the point where one less round in that double-column magazine became a deal breaker. For example, when S&W introduced the so-called Third Generation of pistol in 1988, the 9mms had 14-round magazines. Great—but Berettas, CZs, Stars, and a couple of other makes offered pistols with 15-round magazines. In short order, S&W realized their problem and re-engineered to make 15-rounders. Now, do you really think there is any significant difference between a 14+1 pistol and a 15+1?

I am fully aware that federal law mandates no new magazines with capacities over 10 rounds. It is a BS law like almost everything else the feds have come up with in the way of firearms legislation, but it is the law and we have to comply. All pre-existing mags with greater capacity are grandfathered-in and there are a blue million of them out there. If you really have to have one, go to any gun show and someone will be selling pre-ban magazines. For example, it is perfectly legal to have a Glock 17 pistol made in 1999 and equip it with a 17-shot magazine made in 1993. You can even install a Glock-made two-round magazine extension and have a pistol

with a permissible 19+1 capacity. I have to mention that you will find the second-market magazines to be pricey.

Now, there's nothing inherently wrong with a high-capacity magazine. In untrained hands, they probably do engender a certain amount of ill-advised largesse with the ammo supply—i.e., "spray and pray." Nothing says that you have to waste your shots, and if you take your training at Thunder Ranch or the Gunsite Academy, you will be forcefully instructed not to do so. The high-capacity phenomenon is a function of the automatic pistol. When we all carried revolvers, gunfights were on a level field, but I must point out that even the grand old wheelgun is falling prey to the high-capacity trend, with several current models (in serious fighting calibers) sporting seven-shot and even eight-shot cylinders. We will talk about high capacity a little more later on in the book, but suffice it to say that as a part of the gun selection process, capacity beyond seven or eight rounds is probably excessive and certainly adds to the bulk of the gun.

In Chapter Five we are going to spend a lot of time on different operating or handling systems, so I will comment only briefly at this point. Life-threatening situations are filled with stress and confusion that tend to cause our fine motor skills to deteriorate very rapidly. This is not a time to be working a life-saving implement that needs special attention and complex handling; therefore, the simple gun is the superior gun.

So, what's the best gun? It differs from one shooter to the next, but hopefully everyone will go about choosing one systematically. The best gun is a gun in a caliber that is adequate for personal defense. The next two chapters will go into this matter extensively, so we'll leave it at that. The best gun is light—light enough that you will carry it habitually, summer and winter, light clothing or heavy. It's also as small and compact as possible, because these factors bear on your willingness to have it along and your ability to deploy it quickly. The gun is shaped to conceal easily, but is a good fit to your hand. Your chosen tool should likewise be realistic for your body stance and hand size and have a capacity that doesn't interfere with any of the foregoing. Finally, it should be simple to manage when the dark day comes that finds you fighting for your life.

Defensive Handgun Ballistics

CHAPTER **3**

hat do you want to happen if and when you come under violent criminal attack?

Assume you are legally armed with a handgun and a developed skill in the use of that handgun. You didn't ask for this attack and you damned sure didn't do anything to provoke it. Nevertheless, a criminal attacker is coming at you, displaying a weapon obviously capable of taking your life and announcing his intention to do you harm.

In a sense, you are lucky in that you are getting a warning that gives you a bit of time. Obviously, you have the means of defending yourself and the personal resolve to do so. But *what do you want to happen* when you draw your gun? Hopefully, he will withdraw and leave you in peace. And *what do you want to happen* if he's not intimidated by the threat of your handgun, continues the attack, and forces you to fire?

Indeed, *what do you want to happen?* The question remains, even if our hypothetical scenario is a little contrived. It should be fairly obvious that what you want to happen is for the attack to stop. By custom and code, society recognizes your right to fight in your own self-defense. Every jurisdiction permits self-defense, even if some deny you the right to bear the arms with which to do it. In those enlightened places where the right to go armed has the blessing of society, you can use your gun to protect yourself. But all reactionary rhetoric aside, you do not have the right to run around righting all the wrongs of society. You have the right to defend, not punish, and your intention should be vocalized and practiced as a simple desire to terminate the threat to your person. *What do you want to happen?* You want to stop the fight.

Still, you need to accept some unpleasant truths. Assume you have chosen your gun and ammunition carefully and developed a skill with them via formal training and regular practice. You've done your best under the severe stress of a personal attack, but the tangible result of a desire to stop the fight is going to be a pair of holes in the body of another human being. In contradiction to the popular slogan, neither guns nor people kill people. But bullets do and that is what this chapter is all about—how bullets work to stop fights. It might be seen as unfortunate that we don't yet have the means of doing this without such grave consequences, but we don't. Firing a major caliber pistol at another person in an effort to stop his attack often does exactly that, but it also sometimes kills him in the process. We will not further dwell on this point. Live with it.

Formally, the stuff of this chapter is called terminal ballistics—the study of the interaction of a bullet and the medium of the target. Internal ballistics is the study of what happens inside the gun and exterior ballistics is the study of the bullet in flight. Both of those branches of the science relate to our concerns here only in the sense that they tell us something about how the bullet gets to the target with enough speed to have a meaningful effect. Obviously, the faster a projectile is moving, the harder it will hit. My grandson can throw a football, but so can John Elway; there's no comparison between the speed of the ball as delivered by these two passers.

Science recognizes the results of different impact velocities with a formula by which we can determine the energy delivered to the target. Energy is informally described as the ability to do work. When you depart from the speeding football analogy and go to pistol bullets, you are now dealing with some degree of penetration. But please note that all it takes to defeat the penetration of a handgun bullet into a human body is a few layers of a material called Kevlar— modern body armor. A person equipped with a vest of this miraculous material can absorb several hits from the most powerful handgun cartridges. He may come out of the experience with some bruising, but the vest will stop the various bullets from penetrating into his torso where they would do severe damage. On many occasions, police officers with their Kevlar vests have absorbed multiple hits, returned fire and killed criminal attackers. The vest absorbs the energy of the bullet before it can penetrate and damage vital organs.

And don't ever believe that old saw about pistol hits knocking someone down—never happens.

This proves a couple of things to me. First, a pistol is the worst possible firearm with which to defend one's self. If you were going to a gunfight (and were somehow unable to decline the invitation), taking a pistol would be a huge mistake. In this unlikely hypothetical, I would personally be inclined toward a BAR full of .30-06 soft points or a sawed-off 12-bore pump loaded to the top with #000 buckshot. Pistols simply don't have the power to be offensive weapons (which they would have to be classified if you actually *went* to that gunfight). Handguns are defensive weapons, because the term defensive implies readiness to defend at any time. I can't carry the BAR or the 870 around with me all the time, so I settle for a handgun. The portable nature of a pistol or revolver makes it capable of being there when you need it.

Second, if a few layers of nylon cloth can render a couple of hits from a powerful handgun completely ineffectual by blocking penetration, their energy level isn't high enough. By way of comparison, consider the following. Two hits from a good .45 ACP load will produce some 738 foot-pounds (ft/lbs) of kinetic energy. But two hits from an eight-pellet load of #000 runs to about 3,482 ft/lbs and a couple of .30-06s from the old BAR is a whopping 5,182 ft/lbs. This is not a futile argument for wider use of .30-06s or #000, but rather a way of dramatizing how carefully we must choose our defensive handguns and their ammunition. Circumstances deny us the use of more powerful weapons, but those two hits from a good handgun usually are sufficient to stop a criminal attack. Why? Because street hoodlums usually aren't wearing body armor, so a pair of well-located hits from a handgun will penetrate their torsos.

Penetration is extremely important. It should be obvious that the same pair of hits that were blocked by a vest in one case and penetrated deeply in another had exactly the same energy. So it is not so much that a particular load develops more energy than another but rather how that load transmits its energy to the target. There is another critical factor in this equation, but we will return to that later.

For years, I have watched the tides of

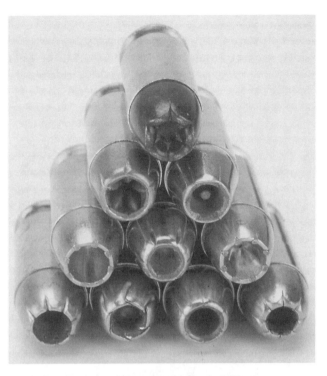

If you are forced to fight, what do you want to happen when you present the gun and press the trigger? Obviously, you want the fight to stop. You want it to be over and done with—as quickly as possible.

There are many different kinds of JHPs in many different calibers. Here are 10 of the best .45 ACPs. Depending on the details of their construction, they will penetrate to various depths and expand to varying diameters.

Guns don't stop fights, but bullets fired from guns do. JHPs once expanded erratically, but modern loads have improved immeasurably in the past 10 years. These are all 230-grain .45 JHPs of various makes, recovered from test media.

A pair (that's right, a pair—always shoot twice) of 230-grain .45 ACP JHPs will deliver 738 foot-pounds of energy. The actual effect on target will be a result of the amount of expansion and depth of penetration. Most of all, the effect will be a function of what organs are hit and how badly they are damaged.

controversy surrounding pistol ammunition ebb and flow. The ammo business is a fiercely competitive one, particularly in view of the vast numbers of cartridges chosen and fired by the nation's police every year. Competition invariably polarizes designers in their search for better ways to do things and designing pistol ammunition is no exception. The result of all this competition is a considerable variety of defensive ammunition, almost all of which is based on one type or another of hollowpoint bullet.

The idea of a hollowpoint bullet is not new. It has been used as least as far back as the time of the UK's big .455 revolvers and the so-called "Manstopper" bullet. That was nothing more than a soft-lead bullet with a huge nose cavity. In modern ammunition, the same idea is used, but with radically different designs. A hollowpoint of any era is intended to deform in tissue and all of

the design effort goes into controlling that deforming process to make the bullet expand regularly. In other words, make the bullet grow in diameter and assume a shape something like a mushroom. The stalk of the mushroom is the original bullet shank, but the cap has blossomed out and grown to much greater diameter than it had when it hit the target medium. The designers have developed the hell out of this simple idea. By varying the shape and depth of the nose cavity, as well as the toughness of jacket and core, bullet engineers can make the bullet expand a little more or little less. They also play with the speed at which the bullet travels in a given load, as they have found out that speed has an effect on expansion.

The effect of increased speed (even a small amount of increase can sometimes have a spectacular effect) is exactly opposite to what you

Just in terms of energy, a handgun is a poor choice for defensive shooting. Here's the data for a pair of hits from 12-gauge eight-pellet #000 buckshot—3,482 foot-pounds, which is roughly 4 1/2 times the energy of a .45 pair.

might think. As we add powder and make a given JHP bullet go faster, it invariably penetrates *less* deeply. That's because the increased velocity tends to make the slug expand faster. Increased rate of expansion means the bullet presents a greater frontal area more quickly and that means the slowing down occurs sooner. I am aware of several instances in which a particular company loads the same bullet to two different velocities. The faster one invariably penetrates less deeply. Interestingly enough, the two recovered bullets appear the same, having expanded to essentially the same shape and diameter.

The ideal balance of expansion and penetration is a controversial matter. But it should be obvious that penetration will occur and that it will happen as a result of the energy developed by the speed and weight of the bullet. How the energy is transmitted to the target is a function of

these two factors, plus the design of the bullet. The temptation is to oversimplify the equation by relying heavily on energy. The formula for calculating energy involves the square of velocity, so the faster the bullet moves, the greater the kinetic energy it will develop. Within the limits imposed by the caliber of the gun and its capacity for propellant, you can achieve some spectacular velocities. Just lower the bullet weight and jack up the velocity and even pussycat cartridges become theoretical tigers. Some firms offer bullets that are so lightly constructed that they expand so violently as to almost explode. This happens almost immediately on impact. Obviously, such a load transmits its energy much differently than a non-deforming FMJ bullet of the same weight and speed. The energy is the same, but instead of a near-total immediate energy transfer, we see a much more gradual delivery of the blow, which

Given a choice, take the shotgun every time. The problem is figuring out a way to pack the sawed-off 12-bore with you all the time. Obviously, you can't do it, so you make the most of the pistol situation.

has a tendency to produce a hole that is considerably deeper and much narrower.

An ultrahigh-speed pistol bullet produces a phenomenon in tissue called a temporary wound cavity. Some observers of the terminal ballistic scene place a great deal of importance on producing as large a temporary cavity as possible. They believe that this ballooning of the wound channel sends pronounced shock waves through an attacker's torso when it is struck by a fast-moving bullet. The theory further holds that this blow will cause the liquids of the body to abruptly move and create such disruption of vital functions that the attacker immediately halts his attack. Blood pressure and respiratory functions are so severely struck that this alone causes an end to the fight. In ammo selection, this theory calls for the loads that deliver the greatest energy possible, and they are almost invariably the fastest ones.

As much as impact velocity certainly is important, another line of reasoning prefers to be a little more cautious. For any given caliber, if you accept a little slower velocity in a somewhat heavier bullet that has been specifically designed for that velocity, you will get a smaller temporary cavity. But you will also get a deeper cavity that is permanent. In most cases, this seems to have a better effect in bringing the fight to a quicker end. Some authorities even go so far to say that you might as well quit worrying about expansion and use an FMJ bullet that always feeds reliably in an automatic pistol. It may produce a through-and-through wound, but if the shot is well-placed, that's enough.

Excessive penetration is clearly undesirable. That's not necessarily because it may produce collateral damage beyond the intended target, but rather because it is wasteful of energy. You pay for that penetration in excessive recoil and muzzle blast when you fire the shot. There's probably not

A defensive shooter needs big bullet holes that are also deep. But most of all, he needs to have them located where they will do the most to stop the fight. A hit with 9mm ball is better than a miss with a .45 JHP. Marksmanship still counts.

a lot of energy left in a bullet that has gone completely through an adversary, but it isn't doing anything worthwhile once it has.

At one point several years ago, most writers on this high velocity versus heavy bullet dichotomy were hard and fast up against one end or the other of the argument. Presently, there seems to be more of a willingness to give a little ground toward the other side's point of view. The ammo makers are also taking everybody's desires into account with several different styles of bullets from each factory—covering all the bases. While the JHP bullets of the '60s and '70s may not have performed well, those of the '90s absolutely do. At one point, I strongly believed that no hollowpoint pistol bullet was moving fast enough to reliably expand, but it's obvious that today's well-designed ones do and some of them at really slow velocities.

While a handgun is far from ideal in a personal defense situation, it is what we are most

likely going to have with us when trouble comes along. When I was making a comparison of handguns and other firearms possibly used in personal defense, I mentioned using pairs of shots. This is not really a terminal ballistics matter, but it has a bearing on understanding the whole subject of defensive handgun use and selection of ammo. We already know that a handgun is not ideal, etc. That's why all of the major handguns schools teach their students to *always* fire two shots in the so-called "hammer" or "controlled pair" technique. They also teach you to assess quickly after the first pair and shoot more shots if there is a need to do so in order to stop the attack. Neither law nor custom insists that you fire one at a time. Why then, would we want to select our ammunition by studying purported statistics on its effect as a one-shot fight stopper?

I have been personally and professionally fortunate in having the chance to attend numerous courses at both Thunder Ranch and Gunsite Academy. Training there has ingrained the two-shot technique so deeply into my subconscious that I have to make a deliberate effort to refrain from pressing that trigger a second time when I am shooting any handgun in any kind of setting. I can do the pair fairly quickly and usually they are pretty close together. The important thing to realize about shooting pairs is not that the second shot *adds* to the effect of the first, but rather that it somewhat *multiplies* it. Properly delivered at common defensive distances, the two shots strike within 2-4 inches of one another. The time interval between the two shots is usually around a quarter of a second and some shooters can do it in close to a tenth. The traumatizing effect of the pair is greater than that of two hits more widely separated in time and location. Developed skill in delivering hammers can take a milder defensive load to an exponentially higher level.

An attack on your person is a serious matter that demands a swift response. Any person who attempts such a thing is your enemy and you are within your rights to destroy him.

There's a saying that applies here: "You destroy your enemy by destroying your enemy." It is unreasonable to expect that, circumstantially limited to a handgun for personal defense, you will get the fight stopped by a simple delivery of as much energy as possible. There's more to it than that. What you need to do is interfere with your attacker's ability to keep up the attack. You might be able to scare him into leaving the field, but don't bet on it. You might also get lucky and encounter an armed robber who has seen two much TV and movies and who believes if he's hit, he has to fall down. This sometimes happens but if you like odds this long, I suggest that you take your paycheck and come to Las Vegas. All you'll lose is your paycheck.

Under criminal attack and resolved to defend yourself, you have no choice but to put some holes in the adversary. Your shots need to produce holes with three characteristics. First, those holes have to be as big a diameter as possible. The better loads will deliver controlled expansion that produces a tissue cavity larger than the bullet's diameter. Second, your hole needs to be as deep as possible. That's right, penetration. Properly

The bullet on the left is a 230-grain Eldorado Starfire, which expands immediately for about 10 inches of penetration. The bullet on the right is a 230-grain Hornady HP/XTP, which expands more slowly and delivers as much as 15 inches.

prepared ordnance gelatin is the accepted standard within the ammo industry and the FBI has done exhaustive testing to determine what is proper for their agent's ammo. By this standard, any acceptable load must produce between 12 and 18 inches of penetration in 10 percent gelatin. Most currently used defensive loads don't go beyond 14 inches. A little more would be better. To the standards of a cavity that's properly wide and sufficiently deep, add a third necessity—your bullet hole must be correctly located. This is not a function of ammo or caliber selection, but rather a matter of marksmanship and tactics. Still, it is something that deserves our attention.

What do you have to hit in order to stop hostile acts by another? The best way to do it is by hitting some part of the central nervous system—either the brain or the spinal cord. Trauma to these vital structures usually causes instant paralysis. But nature placed these organs deep within the body and protected them with tough bone. They're also fairly small and hard to hit. Therefore, sound tactical doctrine teaches us to strike the vital organs that lie high in the human torso. The circulatory and respiratory systems—heart, lungs, and connecting major blood vessels—are vital to continued hostile activity. Bullets delivered to these areas tend to crush vital organs and sometimes cut major blood vessels. The more tissue in the chest you can destroy, the quicker the fight will be over. Penetration of a pistol bullet, compounded with a certain amount of bullet expansion as delivered to vital organs is what stops fights. Penetration is also important in the sense that a defensive shooter often has to shoot through something in order to get to his adversary's torso. That might be auto glass, doors, heavy clothing, and even the bones of an attacker's upraised arm.

It is a grim and unpleasant topic to discuss. But understanding the basics of terminal ballistics in a defensive setting is important. If you fire any of the guns and ammunition discussed here at an attacker and put him on the ground bleeding, the consequences are going to be tough to deal with. But I'll bet you'll find it much easier to handle than you would if you were down and bleeding. Remember, big holes, deep holes, properly located holes.

The Manstopping Calibers—
Plenty of Options

CHAPTER **4**

After the preceding chapter's lengthy discussion of terminal ballistic principles and their implications, it's time to get into some bottom-line numbers. That means an examination of the actual cartridges that deliver the bullets that produce the immediate fight-stopping performance we all would like to have. It should come as no surprise that when you are talking numbers in a discussion of performance, the bigger numbers are the better ones. There are some exceptions, but everything will clear up after we get past some basics.

The caliber of a handgun is the size of its barrel, i.e., the inside diameter of the bore. It is usually given as an English measurement in fractions of an inch—.22, .32, .357, etc. Sometimes, as when the particular cartridge has a European origin, the bore dimension is given in metric terms—6.35mm, 7.62mm, or 9mm. Very often, there is a metric designation for a cartridge that also bears an English name. A 6.35mm Browning is the same cartridge as the .25 ACP. This initial designation tells us something about the cartidge's suitability for defensive use, but not everything. That's why most cartridges also have a name or other descriptive indication beyond just the size of the bore.

With just the number, you would get a pretty good idea of a pistol's worth in the defensive scheme of things, but the additional name really completes the designation. Therefore, knowing that a pistol is a 9mm tells you a lot, but knowing that it is a 9mm Luger tells me that ammo is available in a wide variety of brands, types, and bullet weights. There are lots of 9mms (9mm Browning Long, 9x21mm, 9x23mm, and a number of others), but only a 9mm Luger uses ammunition that is popular around the world because it has been chambered in more different pistols than any other. Bore diameter numbers tell only part of the story; you get the rest from the words. Besides, for one reason or another, there's a lot of downright

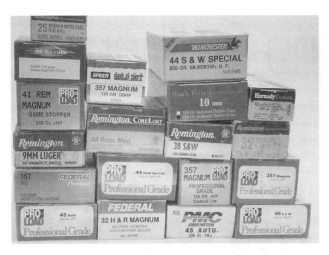

There are many different calibers that would get the job done. And there are even more makers and styles of bullets. The selection process can be complex.

Handgun ammunition rages from the tiny little .25 ACP all the way up to the massive .454 Casull. Neither of these is a good choice for concealed-carry handguns.

Here's an example of how cartridges evolve. The .44 Russian is a frontier-era round from S&W. It evolved into the longer .44 Special cartridge around the turn of the 20th century, then further evolved into the .44 Magnum in the middle part of the last century.

The gun is very old—a S&W Baby Russian—but the ammo is brand new. The .38 S&W will never be loaded to full potential because of the number of older, less sturdy guns still in circulation.

bum scoop involved in bore designations. For example, .38 Specials aren't even .36s when you measure the bore. The micrometer will tell you they are .357s, but if I called them .357 Specials, I would only confuse the issue.

The name of the cartridge tells you what you can logically expect from it. Here's an example. The .44 Russian cartridge (with an actual bore of .429-.430 inch) dates to the black-powder days of the 1870s. A similar cartridge called the .44 S&W Special evolved from it and it has the same bore diameter. So does another one called the .44

Magnum, but there's a world of difference between the three. The difference is a longer case, which results in greater capacity or room for gunpowder. The Russian is nowhere near as powerful as the Special and the Magnum is a lot more powerful than either of its two predecessors. The Russian is only loaded for Cowboy Action Shooting and is rather an ineffectual load. But the .44 Special is enjoying a considerable rebirth of popularity and all ammo makers produce some kind of sensible defensive load for it. While the .44 Magnum certainly has enough power for personal

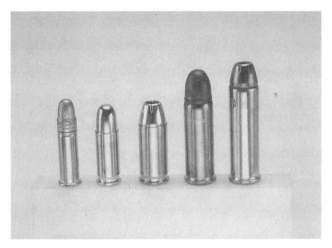

Avoid using these rounds for personal defense. They are just not enough gun: (left to right) .22 Long Rifle, .25 ACP, .32 ACP, .32 S&W Long, and the .32 H&R Magnum.

In revolver cartridges, the lowest power round that is really adequate for defensive work is the century-old .38 Special. Millions of guns have been made for this cartridge.

One current design trend is to make neat little pistols chambered for the .32 ACP round. Just like this old Colt Model M, the guns may be appealing, but the cartridge they deliver is not adequate for personal defense.

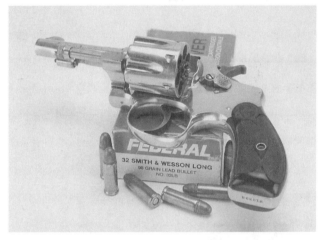

The .32 S&W Long (and shorter .32 S&W) is an old cartridge that is still made because of the number of guns in circulation. Like the .32 Auto, there's insufficient bullet diameter, weight, and velocity to stop fights.

defense, most of the available loads are excessive for the matter at hand. So at least a couple of makers are producing what amounts to hot .44 Special loads in .44 Magnum cases.

Sometimes, the constraints of a gun's mechanism and structure impose limits on how hot the ammo manufacturers can load ammunition for it. The .38 S&W cartridge is a small .36 dating to the early black powder cartridge era. Until recent years, S&W and other makers made some good quality modern arms chambered for this round, but those guns have

gone out of print because of a lack of equally modern ammo to go in them. The ammo companies could easily produce a high-performance .38 S&W load, but they'll never do it. Why? Well, mostly because of the relatively weak guns still in circulation that were made in the infancy of the cartridge.

For one reason or another, some handgun cartridges fall into a range of performance characteristics that make them useful for personal defense use. Others, while useful for some handgun applications, just don't measure up for

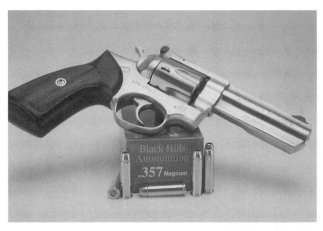

The .357 Magnum has been with us since 1935 and is undeniably the most versatile handgun cartridge of all time. Currently loaded with bullets from 110 to 180 grains, the .357 offers a wide range of velocities. Some of the very best defensive loads are .357s.

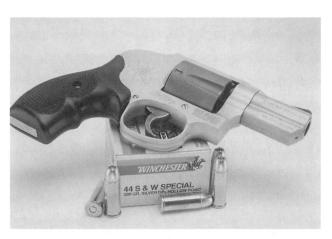

The .44 Special is almost as old as the .38 Special. It has been a cult-favorite round for years. In some of the new lightweight revolvers, the .44 Special is an excellent defensive round.

Here's a pair of rounds that are sometimes endorsed, but are in fact marginal fight-stoppers. The smaller round on the left is the .380 Auto, while the other is the 9x18mm Makarov. Recent imports of thousands of Makarov pistols caused the ammo makers to build ammo. Makarov bullets are about .363-inch in diameter, an odd size common to no other.

In the 1960s, .41 Magnum guns and loads came along. Initially intended to be a police duty cartridge, the .41 quickly became the darling of some sportsmen. Recently, several small .41 Magnum revolvers have given new life to the round. We need a low-velocity, heavy bullet .41 Magnum load.

reasons of performance at one extreme of the spectrum or another. You can have too much power. Such cartridges as the .454 Casull, .475 Linebaugh, .50 Action Express, and most loadings of the .44 Magnum certainly deliver enough of a smack as to end most street fights. But they also deliver serious amounts of penetration, combined with great recoil and muzzle blast. Sure, they'll get the job done, but their designed application is

long-range handgun work on game animals and they have the power for that. It is power that's excessive and it doesn't make for fast pairs. Besides that, all of these monsters come in guns so large that they are impractical for concealed carry. Again, you can have too much gun.

But what is far more likely to happen to a neophyte in the process of picking out a gun and ammo is coming up with too little gun rather than

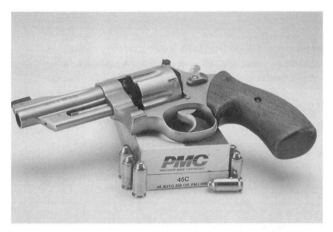

The .45 ACP cartridge is made in great variety and works well in revolvers as well as in the autos. We may even see a compact .45 ACP revolver from Taurus soon. S&W has made six-shot, N-frame .45 ACPs since 1917.

The 9mm cartridge, aka 9x19mm, 9mm Parabellum, or most commonly the 9mm Luger, is the minimum acceptable defensive cartridge for autos. You can get a bunch of them into modern pistols and the resulting gun is easy to shoot.

too much. There are a myriad of guns out there that are so little and so easy to carry—so *cute*, if you will—that even some pretty savvy handgunners rationalize packing them. The current rage is a new generation of .32 ACP pistols that are absolute marvels of packaging. Some are reliable and simple to use. But recall the point made in an earlier chapter, where I said that guns don't stop people, but bullets do. Guns this small have to be chambered for inadequate cartridges in the fight-stopping sense. Proponents of the little rounds often dismiss criticism of their marginal power by advising their owners to perform special shooting tricks like aiming for the eye sockets. If the gun's power is so lacking as to require such dubious technique, the time to change to something better is not when you are under attack, but right now. Choose before the fight.

For this reason, I firmly believe that no .22-, .25-, or .32-caliber handgun cartridge is appropriate for personal defense. The case capacity in the little ones is not adequate to produce enough velocity with any weight bullet. In my book, all of the .22 rimfires, plus the .25 ACP and all common .32 pistol or revolver rounds are improper selections as defensive rounds. Some folks are going to scream in wounded agony at this statement, because it rules out the most powerful .32 cartridge of them all—the .32 H&R Magnum. Some high-quality concealable revolvers from S&W and Ruger have been made

for this little small-game cartridge in the past few years. Nowhere in the handgun scene do we hear that old saw "It's better than nothing!" so often as when the merits of this cartridge are discussed. Only Federal loads ammo for the .32 Magnum, a 95-grain LSWC and an 85-grain JHP. Neither load will develop 200 ft/lbs of energy in a short barrel and neither stands a good chance of stopping a criminal attack. While it may very well be, ah, better than nothin', you can have a gun of the same size with significantly greater power.

The next step up from the .32s are several different cartridges in the 9mm (.355-inch bore) and nominal .38 (.357-inch bore) size. Some of them have enough capacity to drive bullets of reasonable weight to some fairly serious velocities. Others, unfortunately, do not. We have already mentioned the .38 S&W in revolvers but such cartridges as the 9x18mm and 9mm Makarov are close to the low-end threshold in pistol cartridges. And after some consideration and comparison, I have come to the conclusion that the very popular .380 Auto is also inadequate for personal defense. Many writers have repeated the reasoning of the preceding generation of writers by pronouncing the .380 as the minimum acceptable load for personal defense. The ammo makers and their bullet designers have improved the performance of this century-old cartridge via a number of superior loads, but the capacity and bullet weight to make this old one really work is just not there.

One of the great developments of the late 20th century was the .40 S&W cartridge. Just about everybody who makes a pistol chambers it for this round. Bullets range from 135 to 180 grains. Police shootings show the round to be effective.

There have been so many nice .380 pistols made over the years that we have convinced ourselves the cartridge is adequate. It isn't.

So what is? Let's take the small revolver cartridges first and work our way up the line to the big boomers that have been stopping fights ever since the introduction of self-contained metallic cartridges. We'll do this by concentrating on cartridges for which there is an easy availability of a variety of defensive loads. If you can't find good defensive ammo for your gun, there is no real point in having it. Handloads are great for the frequent practice you should be getting, but the loads in your carrying gun need to be fresh factory fodder.

The low-end revolver cartridge that makes the cut is .38 Special. It was introduced with the K-frame S&W revolver in 1899. In short order, the .38 Special and its slim and graceful medium-sized M&P revolver became favorites of American handgunners. For most of the century, the medium frame .38 Special revolver, Colt, S&W, or Ruger, was the almost universal choice of the nation's police. Ammo in .38 Special has been

loaded in bullet weights from 90 to 200 grains and the current variety is almost that wide. You can now find .38 Specials with top-notch JHP bullets weighing from 95 to 158 grains. The best are probably the 125s and 147s. While the .38 has declined in use as a duty firearm for the police, it remains a top choice for use in short-barreled concealed-carry revolvers. In an effort to interject a little more performance into this cartridge, the ammo makers came up with special higher velocity loads called +P ammunition. The effect of this increased power ammo, combined with better JHP bullets and stronger (but lighter) guns, has made today's .38 Special +P a good choice for the defensive shooter.

Every handgunner who has read more than a half dozen issues of *Guns & Ammo* knows the story of the .357 Magnum. It grew out of 1930s-vintage hot .38 Special loads (called .38-44s for .38 loads for use in .44 frame guns) and was formally introduced in 1935. At first, .357 Magnums were all huge guns that were very difficult to carry, but technology brought gun size/weight down to

From the .40 S&W came the .357 Sig, a high-velocity round with bullets from 125 to 150 grains in weight. It is a .40 S&W necked to 9mm for feeding reliability and more case capacity. With bullets of comparable weight, it edges the .357 Magnum.

The unquestioned king of the hill in pistol cartridges is the .45 ACP, which was developed in the early 20th century and retains its popularity into the 21st. Many JHPs are available, but you can make a good case for plain 230-grain Ball.

The 10mm pistol cartridge came along in the mid-1980s and enjoyed a brief run of popularity. It was hard on guns and gunners and eventually lost out to the milder .40 S&W. Only a few guns are still made.

These are the main pistol cartridges for defensive use. From the left they are 9mm Luger, .357 Sig, .40 S&W, and .45 ACP.

today's lightweight five shots weighing as little as 11 ounces. Almost any .357 Magnum load—from the 125-grain snubby loads to the big 180-grain hunting type—is adequate for personal defense. As a rule, you get a little more penetration with the heavier bullets and a little more expansion with the lighter ones. Special 110-grain "snubby" loads also exist, but they give up a lot in order to be comfortable to shoot. Nobody is ill-armed with a .357, which also fires all of the .38 Specials. It is the most versatile of revolver cartridges.

A wheelgun cartridge that tried to give revolver fans what they need for personal defense and police service is the .41 Magnum. Introduced in 1964, the big .41 started behind the 8-ball because S&W put it in a huge N-frame revolver like the .44 Magnums. There was a good police service load with a 210-grain LSWC bullet at about 950 fps, but most ammo was 210-grain JHPs and JSPs at much higher velocities. On those occasions when this stuff was used it worked well, but it delivers excessive recoil and muzzle blast, as

These are the revolver cartridges that make sense for personal defense. From the left, they are .38 Special, .357 Magnum, and .44 Special.

Maybe a little less popular, but nonetheless effective, here are the secondary revolver cartridges. From the left, they are the .41 Magnum, .44 Magnum (some loadings), .45 ACP, and .45 Colt.

well as wasteful penetration. The lower-velocity loads have all disappeared from the scene, but some beautiful new lightweight five-shot defensive guns from Taurus might give the ammo makers a reason to develop a low-recoil JHP defensive load for them. I hope so, but the .41 Magnum is unquestionably a defensive cartridge in decline for lack of enough good loads and guns.

Exactly the opposite is true of the .44 Special. Invented in the early days of the 20th century, the .44 Special became the darling of handloading experimenters like Elmer Keith. Always used in big six-guns from Colt and S&W, the .44 Special went into a downward spiral as an all-around cartridge when the .44 Magnum came along. But an idea came along in the 1970s that gave the .44 Special a new role in the scheme of things. Charter Arms introduced a small five-shot revolver for the .44 Special and other companies—notably Rossi, Taurus, and S&W—followed suit. Current Taurus and S&W .44 Specials are made on a choice of steel or lightweight frames. They are packable revolvers and the ammo makers have a variety of good choices for them. The .44 Special is an old cartridge, but still a useful one in a new generation of small hideout revolvers.

In many ways, the parent .44 Special has more application to the defensive handgun scene than its successor, the more powerful .44 Magnum. While there are several good medium-velocity .44

Magnum loads, the majority of ammo for the big .44s is excessively powerful for reasonable use in a concealed carry handgun. Also, the smallest and lightest .44 Magnum revolver is still enough of a handful to be a major problem in carrying. Most of the time, the .44 Magnum is going to be loaded with .44 Special ammo for personal defense, so why use a heavy gun that has an unused capability? Some rural locales may be appropriate settings for concealed carry with a Magnum, but not many.

How about .45 revolvers? If you can bear the weight and bulk, a .45 ACP revolver is arguably a great defensive handgun and we will look at the cartridge when we take it up under automatic pistols. There's also the grand old .45 Colt, which makes a fine defensive revolver. Taurus now has a .45 Colt snubbie on the same frame as their .41 Magnum and .44 Special. If there is any weakness to the argument for the .45 Colt as a defense gun, it is the poor selection of ammo for this application. There are some bigger revolver rounds, but none are suited for concealed carry. That means it's pistol time.

The smallest pistol cartridge deemed appropriate for use in concealed carry handguns is also the most widely distributed. Since 1902, shooters have used the 9mm Luger cartridge in an enormously diverse range of pistols—and even a few revolvers. It was the standard German pistol

They are less commonly used, but still effective—.38 Super, 9x23mm, and 10mm Auto—all great automatic pistol cartridges.

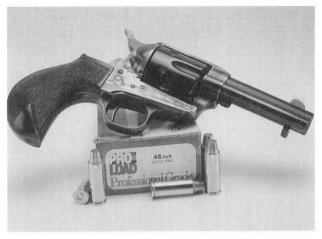

The .45 Colt is a fine old revolver cartridge that we most commonly find in a dated single-action revolver. But in these days of Cowboy Action Shooting, there are a great many handgunners who have learned to manage the older guns, so why not?

cartridge in both World Wars, is the current choice of almost every army in the world and since 1985, is the load that all American armed forces use. In the 1970s, the United States police market went spastic over the 9mm and ammo makers began an intense period of bullet and load development.

There are some big advantages to the 9mm Luger, the most important of which is size. Used in well-engineered small guns, the 9mm Luger absolutely destroys the reasoning behind the much less powerful .380 Auto. Cartridges in 9mm are small enough to neatly stack into a double-wide magazine and still have a fairly small butt on the pistol. They are large enough to have a case capacity that will drive a 124-grain bullet to as much as 1,100 fps and a 147-grain one to 950. Fired with typical loads, 9mm pistols generate modest recoil and almost anyone can shoot one. As rosy as all this might seem, the shooter needs to understand that 9mm power is on the low end; it was the 9mm that caused the two-shot drills to come into modern tactical doctrine.

When the 9mm pistol and its 15-shot magazines wormed their way into wide use, a lot of shooters fought a rearguard action in defense of the .45 ACP and its big, heavy bullet. For a while there, it seemed like there was no way to reconcile the hefty performance gap between the two. Then came SHOT Show 1990 and the Winchester/Smith & Wesson introduction of the

.40 S&W cartridge. This is a completely new cartridge that delivers a 180-grain bullet of .400-inch diameter at 950 fps. While it may have been influenced by the earlier introduction of the 10mm Auto round (which was far less successful), the .40 S&W proved to be a resounding success. Many 9mm-equipped departments immediately went to the .40 and its big bullets. The guns were the same size as the 9mms and held a few less rounds, but produced excellent results in actual shootings. It is probably the most widely used defensive pistol cartridge by a narrow margin (lots of 9mms and .45s are still in use), but is important in the context of this book in that many small .40 S&W pistols are on the market.

The .40 S&W was developed to produce medium velocities with medium-weight bullets of medium-bore size. It was almost inevitable in a velocity-driven market that someone would use that .40 S&W case capacity to drive a lighter bullet to higher velocity. Sigarms (and Federal Cartridge) did it with the .357 Sig cartridge. Essentially, the .357 Sig is the .40 S&W case fitted with a stubby little bottleneck that holds a 125-grain 9mm bullet. This round has sufficient capacity to drive that bullet to as much as 1,400 fps, depending on the load. At this point, velocity begins to have more meaning. A number of major police agencies have adopted the round and any gun that can take the .40 S&W can take the .357 Sig. Sometimes, all that's required is a new barrel. The .357 Sig is a very flat-shooting round that is also extremely accurate. Every ammo maker now offers a load or two for the cartridge and there are even a couple of heavy bullet loads with 147- and 150-grain bullets. Finally, while the .357 Sig has a bottleneck shape unfamiliar to modern handgunners, it feeds as slick as grease—very reliable functioning.

It's probably possible to overstate the affection of American handgunners for the .45 ACP cartridge, but I don't know how. Suffice it to say that the big .45 ACP is America's own combat cartridge and has been for virtually all of the troubled 20th century. There are plenty of reasons why this has come to pass. First of all, the cartridge gets it done. Other rounds may deliver more energy, accuracy, expansion, or penetration, but no other one comes up with so reliable a blend of all of the desirable features of a combat handgun. Old arguments about the .45 pistol being too big to carry and shoot fall apart with the introduction of improved .45 carry guns. The ammo is amazingly varied, with reliably performing JHP bullets weighing from 165 to 230 grains. You can even make a good case for plain old GI 230 FMJ Ball ammo as a proper load for personal defense. No shooter armed with a .45 pistol (or revolver) and good ammunition is ill-armed.

There are a couple of other pistol cartridges that work very well, but just don't seem to attract enough consumer attention to warrant the ammo makers developing a real assortment of high-performance ammunition. The first that comes to mind is the 10mm Auto, which was introduced to us in the early 1980s. It was doing OK by the end of that decade, but it had a reputation for being hard on guns and gunners. It really is an intense cartridge, driving a 200-grain bullet to as much as 1,200 fps. When the FBI adopted it in a problem-plagued S&W pistol, they had their ammo loaded down to about 950 with a 180-grain bullet. That is exactly the performance envelope for the .40 S&W, which quickly shouldered the longer 10mm cartridge out of the way. Like the .41 Magnum in a revolver, the 10mm is maybe a bit too powerful with its hot loadings and it seems to be in a decline, although a couple of excellent Glock pistols are still made in this chambering.

Winchester and Colt got together a few years ago to produce an ammo/gun combination for competition use. Called the 9x23mm Winchester, the new round went in a full-sized M1911A1 pistol and blew the aging .38 Super completely away. It was really a 9mm Luger stretched out to the maximum—4 millimeters longer case—and had a very well-designed strong case. Velocities were in the high 1,400s with a 125-grain Silvertip. The round performed nicely in the gun and made major for the IPSC shooters without any of the pressure problems of hot-loaded .38 Supers. It just never caught the public fancy, although some competitors still use it. Interestingly, I have seen reputable handloading data that shows a much higher velocity potential. If a slightly heavier bullet were to be used, we might have something, but the future doesn't look bright.

While I might want to lobby for something else, the fact remains we do have a respectable assortment of decent calibers and a diverse array of ammunition for them. In revolvers, it's .38 Special (particularly some of the +P loads), .357 Magnum, and .44 Special, with some use of .45 ACP, .45 Colt, .41 Magnum and a few loadings of the .44 Magnum. Autos for the 9mm, .40 S&W, .357 Sig, and .45 ACP get it done. The 10mm, .38 Super, and 9x23mm pistols are not at all bad. That covers the calibers—we'll start on guns in the next chapter.

Handgun Types
and Characteristics

here are two general types of handguns suitable for concealed-carry use: pistols and revolvers. While there are other kinds of handguns, such as the single-shot pistol, their one-round cartridge capacity makes them a poor choice for our consideration. There are also a number of modern double derringers that are certainly small enough and, in many cases, sufficiently powerful for defensive work. But a pair of rounds is just not enough to provide a margin of error in combat shooting. Consequently, we choose between either a pistol or a revolver. In this chapter, we will look at the characteristics, advantages, and disadvantages of both classes of handguns.

Revolvers have seniority in the chronological evolution of fighting handguns and that's reason enough to look at them first. Advanced students of firearms have found a number of instances of multi-chambered firearms that predate the products of Samuel Colt, but nobody seems to disagree that Colt was the first to offer repeating, revolving cylinder handguns on a mass-production basis. His idea was said to have evolved from his experiences as a young seaman watching the spokes of the ship's wheel. Whatever inspired the concept, it has proven to be a very logical and durable one. The company that bears his name still exists and still makes a handgun that is mechanically no different than the Colt revolvers of 1836.

The earliest Colts were cap-and-ball firearms, where powder and bullet were inserted in each firing chamber of the cylinder. The chambers were closed at the rear and a percussion cap was fitted to a nipple that was struck with the tip of the gun's hammer in order to fire. This system made an easy transition to completely self-contained metallic cartridges as soon as Colt was legally able to use this new system. The real essence of the revolver concept was the idea of a drum-like cylinder holding several firing chambers, each

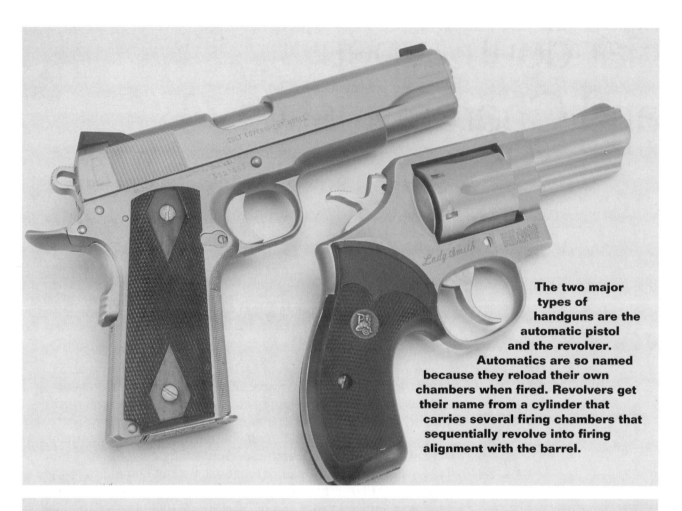

The two major types of handguns are the automatic pistol and the revolver. Automatics are so named because they reload their own chambers when fired. Revolvers get their name from a cylinder that carries several firing chambers that sequentially revolve into firing alignment with the barrel.

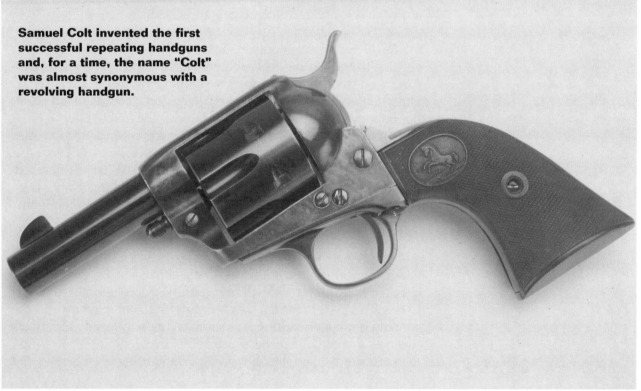

Samuel Colt invented the first successful repeating handguns and, for a time, the name "Colt" was almost synonymous with a revolving handgun.

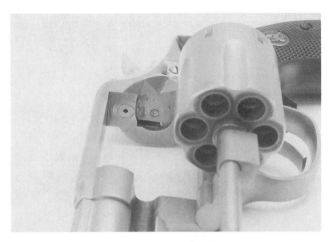

Looking at this modern S&W handgun with its cylinder open, you can see a slot (center of the picture) where a "hand" reaches through and engages a ratchet (out of sight) and turns the cylinder.

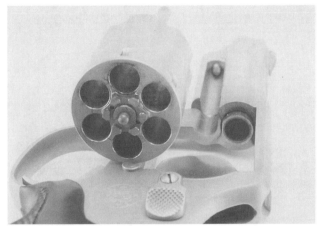

Here's the rear of the same cylinder, showing the ratchet, which the hand turns to make the gun work. The concept is as old as the first Paterson Colt revolver of 1836. It stills works and hundreds of thousands are made annually.

Here a single-action (SA) revolver as made by Ruger. The terminology describes the nature of the trigger, where pressure causes a single thing to happen. The shooter must manually cock the hammer; pressing the trigger makes it fire.

This S&W revolver is a double action/single action (DA/SA). Once again the name describes the trigger action(s). Trigger pressure causes two things to happen: (1) cocks or loads the hammer, (2) releases it to fire. In the alternative, he may manually cock the hammer and press the trigger to fire.

of which is spaced equally around the central axle on which the cylinder rotates. As each chamber revolves into alignment with the fixed barrel, a part of the mechanism locks that alignment securely in place. Barrel-cylinder alignment is essential in a working revolver, since even the slightest misalignment will cause the bullet to hit the edge of the barrel as it exits the cylinder throat to make the crossing to the forcing cone of the barrel.

What happens in a revolver is simplicity itself, but what makes it happen can be pretty complicated. The mechanism of the revolver generally works off a hammer that swings through a short arc to whack the primer in the base of the cartridge. Levers working off that hammer as it moves to the rear (or "cocks") must reach up and turn the cylinder into proper alignment with the barrel, but also must activate a sturdy little lug that eases into a recess on the outer circumference of the cylinder to lock it in place at the instant of firing. All of this must happen at exactly the same moment—timing is critical and a revolver that doesn't do it is said to be "out of time." When you

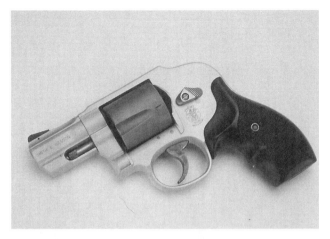

This S&W .44 is a specialized variation called a double-action only (DAO) where the internal hammer cannot be manually cocked and every shot must be through a long arc, dynamic trigger pull that both raises the hammer and releases it to fire the gun.

Most automatic pistols like this Sig P239 9mm have a provision to lock the slide back when the last round is fired. The slide (top half of the gun) moves back and forth on rails.

The so-called "automatic" pistol comes in many varieties, sizes, and types. When the gun fires a shot, the mechanism cycles in such a way that the fired round extracts from the chamber and ejects from the gun. The gun then feeds another round into place to be fired and readies the trigger mechanism to make it happen. This Sig P230 .380 is a blowback pistol that does not require a breech lock mechanism.

Here's the same gun with the slide forward. As a 9mm, the pistol is recoil-operated via the Browning system. When the pistol fires, the slide and barrel are locked together and move rearward together a short distance. An internal cam arrangement under the barrel causes the two parts to separate, which allows the slide to move completely to the rear.

consider the incredible beating a working revolver takes, it's amazing that such a subtle system works as well as it does.

But a properly working revolver as made by one of the current major manufacturers does indeed work and with remarkable simplicity. With skillful guidance, the most inexperienced neophyte can be introduced to a revolver and find himself shooting it effectively in a very short period of time. It's all happening right in front of his eyes—he can see the cylinder open to reveal the firing chambers and their cartridges, he can see how the cylinder closes and how the turning motion of the cylinder relates to the rearward movement of the hammer. And it becomes immediately obvious that when the hammer falls and the gun fires, repeating the manipulation of hammer and trigger will make it happen again. But it is also instantly apparent

The trigger system on this little Kimber is the time-honored Browning single action. The only logical way to work this gun is to carry it with the hammer cocked and the manual safety in the "on" position. This makes some people unnecessarily nervous.

On this Sig P220, the first shot is DA, but subsequent shots are SA. It is a useful way to work a gun. Even more to the credit of designers, the gun is fitted with a well-located decocker on the frame. There's no safety and no need for one.

that opening the cylinder removes the unfired cartridges from their relationship with the rest of the gun. It is very easy to make it safe.

These characteristics of the revolver cause a fundamentally archaic mechanism to retain popularity in a world that is infatuated with technology. And make no mistake about it, modern technology applied to the building of the old mechanism results in the most accurate and dependable revolvers ever built. For those seeking a dependable defensive handgun, a revolver is a completely effective and often economical option that deserves serious consideration. There are several different types of revolvers that we need to understand before we leave the subject of the wheelguns.

Revolvers are broadly divided into two different types: single action and double action. In truth, the two terms apply to the nature of the triggers used in the guns and not to the guns themselves. In pure form, "single action" means a trigger system where trigger pressure performs a single function—releasing the hammer to fire the handgun. Typical guns using a single-action trigger are the many types of Rugers, as well as Colt Peacemakers and their many replicas. Firing them requires manual cocking of a hammer that is well-shaped for the purpose. This is the original type of trigger and the system is associated with the revolvers of the Western frontier period.

At about the same time Sam Colt was producing his first guns in New Jersey, another inventor obtained a patent for a simple single-shot pistol with a spurless tube hammer. He called the trigger on this gun "double-acting" because trigger pressure performed two functions: it raised the hammer to a cocked position and released it to fire. Over the following decades, most revolvers had single-action triggers, but a few used double-action ones also. Modern guns almost exclusively have two types of triggers incorporated into their lockwork systems. This has confused many writers into describing such guns as double action because they may be fired both ways. A more precise term would be DA/SA, an abbreviation for "double action, single action." There is another type of mechanism found on some of the best of modern hideout revolvers and it has confused the issue even more. Some revolvers eliminate the cocking function on the hammer and resort to a simple sweep-through double-action pull and are known as DAO (double-action only). It's important to understand the differences, because the trigger terminology has crept over into automatic pistols as well.

Revolvers have major advantages in modest initial cost, simplicity of operation, and an excellent ratio of gun weight and bulk to power. Their disadvantages are relatively slow reloading time, fairly low capacity (most commonly it's five

This S&W auto has what the company calls a traditional double-action (TDA) trigger system. The first shot is dynamic double action, but when the action cycles, the hammer stays cocked for a second shot in single action. The lever on the slide will drop the hammer safely and prevent any trigger movement.

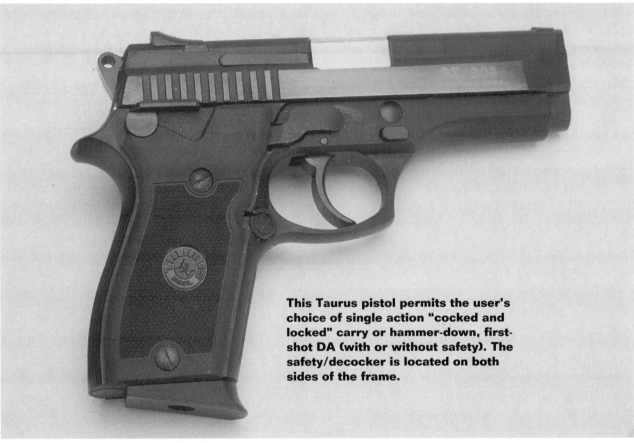

This Taurus pistol permits the user's choice of single action "cocked and locked" carry or hammer-down, first-shot DA (with or without safety). The safety/decocker is located on both sides of the frame.

or six shots), and considerable bulk in the more powerful calibers. In my view, their greatest advantage is simplicity of operation. A current production DAO or DA/SA revolver can be remarkably compact, surprisingly powerful, and utterly simple to manage. The old wheelgun is not all that far from two centuries of honest service to handgunners and they can still get the job done. Simply put, revolvers stop fights.

The same is true of the other type of handgun, the automatic pistol. I believe that the terminology of "automatic" pistol derives from the gun's unique ability to automatically reload its own chamber and has nothing to do with the trigger system or operating system. There have been— and currently are—a few pistols that have fully automatic operating systems, where one press of the trigger will produce repeated shots until the pressure is relaxed or the ammo is exhausted. Legally classified as machine guns, they require Federal registration and taxing, but are probably impractical anyway. Most of the pistols we casually refer to as autos or automatics are legally seen as semiautos, in that a single press of the trigger produces one shot and another press is necessary for the next one.

Practical pistols date to the turn of the century. In a few short years, a number of successful pistols came into being. Initially a number of ideas were employed to get the pistol to fire high-pressure ammunition safely. Designers quickly determined that if the gun's mechanism was going to reload itself, it had to open and close as successive shots were fired. If the intensity of the shot was from a fairly low-pressure cartridge, the breech could be held closed briefly by the weight of the recoiling parts and the strength of the recoil spring. This came to be called "blowback" operation and it worked OK for cartridges up to the .380 Auto. But try anything with more zip and the need for a mechanical lock became quickly apparent.

For that reason, John Browning and other designers of that era came up with various forms of recoil operation. The term comes from the use of the pistol's inherent recoil movement to unlock some form of mechanical breech lock. Toggle locking systems and internal breech blocks were used, as well as later pivoting locking blocks and turning barrels, but the most common was the tilting barrel system. In this system, the barrel and slide are locked together at the instant of firing. Locked together, they recoil a short distance until the bullet exits the barrel and breech pressure drops. At this point, either cams under the barrel or a tethered link cause the rear of the barrel to drop, unlocking it from the slide. The barrel stops, but the slide continues rearward to extract the fired case and eject it from the gun. When the rearward movement stops, the compressed recoil spring expands and drives the slide forward, an action that also feeds a cartridge from the magazine into the barrel's firing chamber, then relocks the barrel to the slide. In this way, the system harnesses the natural thrust of recoil to make the gun work for repeated shots. With a few notable exceptions, every pistol mentioned in the following chapters of this book is recoil-operated.

Since most practical defensive pistols are recoil-operated, the shooter has no real option in choosing one over the other. But he has a considerable range of options in the handling characteristics of the various makes and models. Designers set up their guns with a bewildering array of different controls that make them easy and safe to carry, handle, and fire. There is just no way out when it comes to understanding these things. You simply have to memorize how your chosen pistol is equipped and work from there. Handguns are, by design, deadly weapons, so you want to be sure you can handle yours safely to avoid negligent discharge. But you want to be equally sure you can get the gun working quickly when it is needed. Let's see if we can get a handle on the basic differences in automatic pistol styles.

First and arguably foremost, there is the oldest system in continuous production. It is the single-action auto with exposed hammer and manual safety. Best exemplified in the eternally popular Government Model .45 pistol of 1911, the SA auto is very simple to manage and quite fast in trained hands. It is in production by the original maker and has been imitated worldwide, as well as outright copied. The most sensible way of carrying the SA auto is with hammer cocked (which makes many people very nervous) with the manual safety "on" or locked. To fire, the shooter draws the gun and depresses the safety with the thumb of the shooting hand, placing his finger on the trigger only as he has his sights aligned on a proper target. Some four pounds of trigger pressure fires the gun. It is the simplest and fastest way to put an automatic pistol into action. With proper training, most handgunners get the hang of it quickly. The shooter must make proper handling of the SA auto an absolute habit, particularly as to reapplying the safety when the gun is not going to be immediately fired. Proper locating of the safety on the receiver of the pistol is critical to smooth and easy use of this kind of gun. If the lever is on slide, as it is in some guns, it is awkward and harder to use.

That's part of the problem with another different type of pistol system. Call this one a DA/SA auto with a combination safety and decocker. These guns have both types of triggers built in. Using a dynamic, long arc double-action trigger for the first shot, this gun leaves the hammer cocked and affords a shorter, static SA trigger for following shots. Depending on the shape of the gun and the way it fits the shooter's hand, there may be a problem in using two different types of trigger pull, i.e., transitioning from one to the other. To allow the shooter to safely lower the hammer, there's a decocking lever and safety on the slide. Reach up and turn it down to decock the pistol. This also activates the safety. Shooting with the gun in this condition requires the shooter to flip the safety up, which seems to be an awkward movement for most shooters. The reason that all of this got started in the first place is a belief that the revolver-like DA first-shot trigger pull is safer and easier, which is probably true.

If it is, then another system might be more appealing to you. This is also a DA/SA, but the decocker is on the receiver or frame of the pistol and it has no safety function. With a loaded chamber and the hammer down, simple DA trigger pressure will raise the hammer and release it to fire. The moving slide cocks the pistol for the next shot, which will be a crisp SA one. If the gun is well-shaped and the decocker is well-located, the use of this control is simplicity itself. There's no manual safety and there is no more need for one than there is on a typical revolver. Handling safety is inherent in good training and practice, plus accepting the revolver-like DA trigger pull as safe in its own right. If this is not sufficiently comforting to you, there are a couple of models

that offer a decocker and safety, but locate them on the frame and make them work "up to safe, down to fire."

The Glock system involves a unique trigger action that has been both imitated and modified. BATF-classified as a DAO, this is a trigger that requires no manual safety. The company calls it "Safe Action" because the trigger is the only operative control. It uses the movement of the slide to partially cock an internal striker. Trigger pressure applied in the act of firing finishes the cocking action, then releases the striker to fire the gun. Appealingly enough, the trigger action is exactly the same from shot to shot. This avoids possible problems in transition from one shot to the next. A number of designs using variations of this DAO system are available. Some of them have safeties worked into the system.

Another DAO variation avoids the precocking or partial cocking of the striker in favor of a revolver-like complete trigger cocking of the entire system. Adherents of this variation feel this is desirable in that it allows a second strike on a misfire. Common sense and good tactical training should tell you to remove a misfired cartridge from your pistol as quickly as possible and get back in the fight. While this brief description of the autos, hits the high spots, there are other models out there that deliver efficient and safe handling with all kinds of lockwork options. Whatever gun you choose, go for whatever fits you and your safety needs, but remains fast to deploy and fire.

In the following chapters of this book we will look at most of the major options in pistols and revolvers. Wherever possible, we'll show them to you in such a way as to make comparisons possible. This means displayed on a square to give you an idea of the gun's size (height and length) plus its weight with a full load of appropriate ammunition. You don't carry a concealed-carry firearm empty and might be surprised to see how quickly the beautiful little gem viewed at the gun store counter becomes a brick when loaded full.

Arbitrarily, I have classified autos as small, medium, and large. The small ones have small frames and barrels around 3 inches in length, the mediums usually sport a little larger (and often high-capacity) frame and barrels of about 4 inches in length. Large autos have barrels longer than 4 inches, but seldom over 5. Their actual frame sizes

Glock calls their guns Safe Action but the BATF import criteria classify them as DAOs. The trigger pull is remarkably short and can be varied in weight by simple substitution of internal parts. The highly popular Glocks have the same pull for every shot and require slide movement to set the trigger system.

This Taurus Millennium .45 ACP is a DAO that requires no slide movement to activate the trigger system. It is a very straightforward and easy-to-use mechanism. Only a few other autos have this kind of lockwork.

vary extensively. Where revolvers are concerned, we also went to a small, medium, and large system. The little 2-inchers with small frames are the small ones and mediums have longer barrels around 3 inches, plus frames either small or medium in size. The relatively few large revolvers suitable for concealed carry have bigger receivers and barrels around 4 inches long.

Small Autos

CHAPTER 6

They're really rather new on the handgun scene. The phenomenon of the small automatic pistol, at least in one of the several calibers we have identified as adequate for personal defense, is a recent one. Driven by the current interest in concealed-carry handguns, firearms makers worldwide have devoted a great deal of time and money to producing compact and carryable handguns that have barrels around 3 inches in length and therefore fall into our arbitrarily established "small" category. It's interesting to note that not one of the guns we'll examine in this chapter existed 10 years ago. Indeed, most of them were introduced within the past five years. That's a pretty good indication of widespread and contemporary consumer interest.

Naturally, some of them are smaller and lighter than others, but none (OK, *almost* none) are so large or heavy that they could not ride in a coat or trousers pocket and be reasonably comfortable for the user. The widespread use of light materials, usually polymer or advanced aluminum alloys, in small guns has been the most significant feature of modern handgun design. Titanium alloys applied to handguns came into prominence right at the tag end of the 20th century. Taurus was the first company to manufacture a pistol slide of the wonder stuff. It's light, it's strong, and we are going to see a lot more of it.

How the light weight is accomplished isn't really the question, though. The fact that guns are lighter and smaller than ever has had an effect on what we are now carrying. For most of the 20th century, the handgunner who wanted something really small and light in an automatic pistol was forced to use a demonstrably inadequate caliber. Usually it was a .380 Auto, sometimes a .32 ACP or .25 ACP. With the introduction of such guns as the Kahr Micro or Taurus Millennium, a shooter can now enjoy a pistol chambered for the powerful 9mm cartridge, but one that's about the same size as the

The smallest of the small autos are small indeed. This is the Kahr Micro, which may be the best pocket auto ever offered for sale.

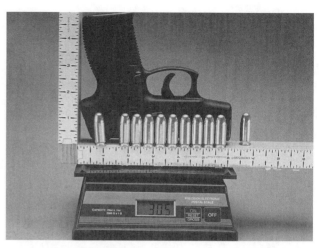

The loaded weight of the 10+1 Taurus Millennium in .45 ACP is 30.5 ounces. The frame is light polymer, but the weight of 11 rounds of 230-grain ammo runs up the total.

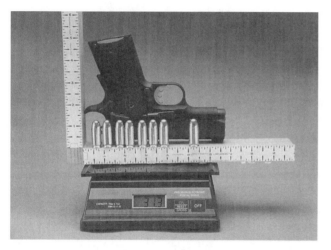

Kimber's smallest is a variation of the venerable Government Model pistol, with short slide and butt. All steel, the gun's loaded (6+1 rounds) weight is 31.3 ounces.

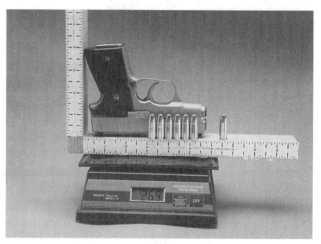

The slick little Kahr Micro is all steel, so the loaded weight is 26.9 ounces. There is also a lightweight polymer version.

best .380s of days gone by. Indeed, the new 9mms are even better in the sense that many of them are extremely small, but incorporate magazines with capacities of up to 10 rounds. That means we have pistols in the size/weight range of traditional .380s, but with magazines holding more rounds than the early full-sized 9mm pistols—Lugers, P38s, S&W M39s. Under these circumstances, why would anyone want to settle for less power or less capacity—or both?

There are also some mighty handy little pistols in the same size class as the 9mms, but

they fire such hot new rounds as the 10-year-old .40 S&W or 6-year-old .357 Sig. Clearly, 21st century handgunners have more choices in better guns for personal defense than ever before. It would almost seem that it's time for them to put aside the wondergun of the 20th century—the venerable and much-loved M1911A1 .45 automatic—in favor of something little and cute and, well, *modern.*

Don't bet on it. The grand old gun lives on in original format and many smaller variations. As a matter of fact, one of the clear design trends of the

In today's competitive handgun market, just about everybody who makes any kind of Government Model pistol makes one of these—a short butt, short slide .45 ACP type pistol. This one is the excellent Kimber Ultra Carry.

AMT started a trend several years ago with a small DAO pistol in .45 ACP caliber. All stainless steel, the gun was rugged but had a heavy trigger pull that drew unwarranted criticism.

Heritage Arms in Florida offers this unique little polymer-framed 9mm (also made in .40 S&W). Another DAO, the gun uses a South African-designed gas-retarded blowback operation that works.

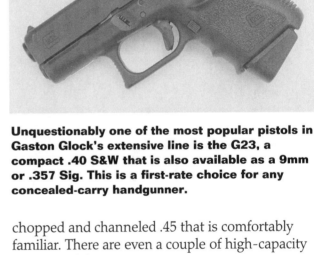

Unquestionably one of the most popular pistols in Gaston Glock's extensive line is the G23, a compact .40 S&W that is also available as a 9mm or .357 Sig. This is a first-rate choice for any concealed-carry handgunner.

last decade has been the miniature M1911. Kimber and Springfield both offer such a pistol, as do a great many custom shops. Just before Colt suspended regular production of pistols in late 1999 they offered a slick little gun called the Defender. It was an Officer's ACP receiver fitted with a special bushingless slide and 3-inch barrel. The Defender worked quite well and a limited numbers of the guns still trickle out of the Colt Custom Shop as the Defender XS. For those who favor that established cocked-and-locked system of defensive handgun carry, you can have a

chopped and channeled .45 that is comfortably familiar. There are even a couple of high-capacity versions of the gun.

With that preamble, we need to get into the meat of the matter—the small automatic pistol. Taking them alphabetically, the first one up is from **AMT** (Galena Industries in Sturgis, South Dakota, has purchased the rights to the AMT line). This American-made pistol called the DAO Backup is attributable to the design genius of Larry Grossman at Harry Sanford's old Arcadia Machine & Tool Company. The pistol came out in the early

By deliberate design, all Kahr pistols are small autos that are top choices in concealed carry handguns. This one is the new lightweight (polymer receiver) P40.

This photo shows the relative sizes of the Micro, Covert, and full-size Kahrs. They are rugged, dependable, and shootable pistols.

Kel-Tec's P11 is an exceptionally light (just over 14 ounces unloaded weight) polymer double-column DAO 9mm and .40 S&W. It is also modestly priced. Further, the gun uses S&W-type magazines.

In a very few short years, the Kimber pistols have become exceedingly popular. This little .45 is like all Kimbers in the sense that it is very well made.

1990s and initially only in .45 ACP. Now the pistol may be had in several other calibers—.357 Sig, .38 Super, 9mm Luger, .40 S&W, and .400 Cor-Bon. At 23 ounces empty, the pistol is rather heavy. However, the designer was smart enough to produce the gun with a positive and simple DAO trigger system, as well as a round-topped slide profile. This latter feature should be on all modern hideout autos, as it ensures the gun will not print through clothing like the typical squared-off modern pistol. Most shooters don't like the heavy trigger, but it's part of the operating system, as

well as something that demands a positive effort in order to fire.

Beretta of Italy is riding high with a lengthy series of service autos, both large and medium in size. But until recently and with the introduction of the gun at hand, they had no pistol in the small defensive pistol category. This newest pistol is the Model 9000 Beretta and it follows the modern trend to 9mm and .40 S&W, as well as polymer receiver and steel upper. Like many Berettas, the little guns of the 9000 series have open top slides. However, they do not have the typical Beretta

While this Para-Ordnance P10 is the company's first little auto, it is not the only one. The Canadian-based firm currently offers a small single-column pistol with their new LDA trigger.

Republic Arms is in California's "Gun Valley" and sells this excellent DAO .45 with simple trigger and polymer frame. The pistol is priced competitively.

pivoting locking block system, or even the turning barrel of the 8000 series guns. Instead, the Beretta designers made an ingenious application of the Browning-originated tilting barrel system. This one differs in the sense that locking surfaces are to the side of the barrel, rather than under it. Guns in this series are made with a choice of either traditional DA/SA trigger systems or DAOs. With 10-shot magazines and barrels close to 3 1/2 inches long, 9000 series Berettas crowd the little gun envelope a bit, but they operate with typical Beretta smoothness.

When **Colt** introduced the Defender pistol in 1998, it was the latest incarnation of the gun that is most closely identified with American handgunning—the Government Model .45 pistol. It also serves as a replacement for the problem-plagued Officer's ACP model Colt. The Defender uses the short ACP receiver, but has a shorter slide with a 3-inch barrel and no bushing. Officer's ACP bushings regularly broke and simply dispensing with them and going to a reverse-tapered or cone barrel solves the problem. There are still timing problems associated with a 3-inch barreled 1911-type pistol, however, and the shooter who chooses one of these guns (regardless of who makes it) had best plan on doing a fair amount of shooting to ensure that his specimen works with regularity. Still, it is an appealing little package that handles and functions in the old and proven way.

Glock of Austria makes defensive autos in three different sizes and the smallest ones fall into our small auto category. Probably no other pistol epitomizes the modern gun as does the reliable Glock. Scarcely 15 years old, Glocks were the first to use the polymer (plastic) receiver construction. This really caught the public fancy, but Glock should be respected more for its innovative lockwork, a feature that sparks unending imitation. It's a form of DAO that feels a little like a single action, but has a trio of passive internal safeties that makes for as safe, but simple to operate, a gun as you'll ever find. Glock's three small autos are really the same pistol in three different chamberings: the Model 26 is a 9mm, the Model 27 is a .40 S&W and the Model 33 fires .357 Sig ammo. All have double-column magazines of 9 or 10 rounds. Although all three pistols are thick enough to constitute a concealment problem, they have many fans and are widely distributed.

By the tiniest bit of stretching, I can squeeze all of the pistols made by **Kahr Arms** into the small-auto category. Like the just-mentioned Glocks, Kahrs have a simple, no manual safety system of DAO lockwork. It's one of the systems whereby the action of the moving slide partially cocks the internal striker, so that dynamic trigger pressure has somewhat less to do to fully load the striker pressure and fire the gun. Kahrs are amazingly trim. They have single-column magazines and are very flat and concealable. Best of all, Kahrs are exceptionally well made, using a small number of strong steel parts. The Kahr variety includes the original K9 and K40, which have longer barrels running to 3 1/2 inches and six- or seven-shot magazines, the smaller and shorter Mk9 and Mk40 and the new lightweight K9 Polymer. The latter gun weighs a whispery 17.9 ounces, but stays a 7+1 9mm hideout. Kahrs are high-quality pistols, often the choice of professionals.

If you want a real lightweight automatic pistol that still has power and capacity, take a look at the **Kel-Tec** P11. Another polymer-frame DAO, the Kel-Tec has a hammer, not the more common striker. It's a continuous DAO, where repeated trigger pressure will continue to smack a recalcitrant primer (if that's what the shooter wants to do). The Kel-Tec has an ingenious receiver, which houses a doublewide magazine of 10 rounds. The upper end of that magazine duplicates the contours of the S&W Third Generation magazines. That means a shooter can use a S&W magazine in an emergency. Therefore, while the P11 comes with a 10-round magazine, it can also use S&W original 12-, 14-, 15-, and 20-shot magazines, which will of course stick out the bottom of the gun. I haven't worked with a Kel-Tec in any caliber but 9mm, but that is a pretty satisfactory little package that weighs only about 14 ounces empty.

Only a few years ago, nobody had heard of a **Kimber** .45 pistol. Today, they are one of the two major makers of Government Model autos. Their catalog is extensive and one model falls into the small auto category. It's called the Ultra Carry. This little pistol is an aluminum-frame .45 ACP in the same general style as the Colt Defender. Like all of the diverse line of Kimber .45s, the Ultra Carry comes with excellent sights, a decent trigger pull,

Sigarms offers versions of their flat P239 in .357 Sig and .40 S&W, as well as the original 9mm caliber. The gun uses a single-column magazine to increase concealability.

S&W's new line of Chiefs Specials includes this chunky CS45, which is a cut-down version of the popular Third Generation pistol called the 4506.

Using the same frame as the .45 Chiefs Special, S&W came up with this CS40 in .40 S&W. The action and lockwork are pure Third Generation TDA.

When it comes to pure packing, the 9mm version of the Chiefs Special auto carries a great deal easier than its bigger brothers in .40 and .45.

and first-rate reliability. Kimbers are always good buys, so if your tastes run to the Government Model .45 ACP pistol in miniaturized form, this is your gun.

Not so many years ago, **Para-Ordnance** was a new firm in the world of handgun manufacturing. Their first product was a widebody kit that allowed a shooter to assemble a high-capacity (14+1) pistol using plain GI parts and the Para receiver and magazine.

In time, the company exploited the success of their kits and offered complete pistols. Their 2000 catalog shows a diverse assortment of widebody

.45 ACP pistols, including the gun at hand, the P10. This is a short-barreled pistol in the M1911A1 style, but fitted with a short receiver that accepts a widebody magazine of 10 rounds. The resulting gun is a chunky little auto with abbreviated receiver and 3-inch barrel and slide. True enough, the high-cap magazine makes for a pistol that's thick in the extreme, but few guns pack so much power into such a small envelope.

Republic Arms is a new company located in California's "Gun Valley" near Chino. Formed to produce a new compact .45 pistol, the firm is doing quite well with a gun called the Patriot. Based on a

Here's the lineup of Taurus Millennium autos. The calibers run from .32 to .45. All in the series have the same type of DAO trigger, plus polymer receivers.

The Taurus 9mm Millennium pistol comes with your choice of carbon steel, stainless steel, or titanium slides.

This is the author's choice as the best small concealed-carry auto in the Taurus line and one of the top two or three guns of any make. It's a 10+1 DAO .45 ACP.

Small autos are one of the better choices for concealed carry and this little Kimber is a great specimen of the breed.

molded polymer receiver and steel upper, the Patriot is a striker-fired gun with a DAO trigger system. It's about as simple as they come, but extensive shooting with two samples on hand tells me the gun is as reliable as it is simple. It's also blessed with very nice ergonomics and, sensibly enough, functions with a lightly modified M1911A1 magazine. One of the better features of the gun is its surprisingly reasonable price tag. Patriots are great choices for the shooter who needs a solid defensive handgun and faces a tight budget.

SIGARMS is located in Exeter, New Hampshire, where they import firearms from Germany and Switzerland and also do a certain amount of finish production of some models. There are a number of pistols in the Sig Sauer series, but only the "flat Sig," the model P239, comes close to our small auto category. This model comes in 9mm, .357 Sig, and .40 S&W. It is a single-column DA/SA pistol with the lockwork system of virtually all pistols of this make. In my opinion, it is the very best way to set up a pistol to have the best of both worlds—a smooth dynamic trigger for the first DA shot and the crisp static SA trigger break for second and subsequent shots. There are no manual safeties on the Sigs and no need for them. There is a beautifully located decocking lever that allows the shooter to safely drop a cocked hammer when tactical circumstances demand it. It is sensible, logical, and, when fitted to a flat little pistol like the P239, produces a fine gun in a choice of potent calibers.

Nobody gives you more handgun choices than **Smith & Wesson**, the legendary arms maker from Springfield, Massachusetts. In small autos, S&W offers three very nicely designed and finished pistols in the three most popular automatic pistol calibers—9mm, .40 S&W, and .45 ACP. Called the CS9, CS40, and CS45 respectively, these relatively new guns are the company's automatic pistol response to their eternally popular Chiefs Special .38 Special, and .357 Magnum revolvers. (The "CS" designation stands for Chiefs Special.) Reduced-size versions of their basic Third Generation automatic pistols, these three autos have 3-inch barrels and what S&W calls "Traditional Double Action" lockwork. The 9mm gun is a bit smaller than the other two, since it uses a smaller, lighter slide than the two bigger calibers. With S&W's excellent lifetime warranty system and quality reputation, the guns are good choices.

Along with Kimber and to some unknown degree, Colt, **Springfield, Inc.** dominates in the 1911-style pistol market. Their colorful catalog lists a whole bunch of different guns in that familiar format. For our purposes here, consider both regular and high cap versions of the little 3 1/2-inch pistols that have exploded in popularity in the past few years. Springfield has them in both blue steel and stainless versions, with compensated barrel/slide units or original plain ones. It's becoming increasingly common for major handgun makers to have in-plant custom shops that will do various types of custom work on their guns. Springfield has a very active shop of this sort.

Finally, take a look at **Taurus International.** For many years, Taurus made low-cost options to pricier pistols and revolvers. Those days are long gone. Taurus guns are as good as anyone's and far better than most. That includes their Millennium series of small autos. Yet another polymer-and-steel DAO pistol, the Millenniums come in 9mm, .40 S&W, and .45 ACP. The trigger is extremely smooth and the gun is fitted with a down-to-fire safety on the frame. I've worked with the 9mm extensively and it is a really nice little pistol. The .45 ACP is a little larger, but is still small enough to ride in a pocket or waistband holster. Doublewide magazines are available on all models. Also it is in the Millennium pistols that Taurus makes yet another technical breakthrough; for greater weight savings, the 9mm versions will be available with ultra-strong titanium slides. That is going to really be popular.

Small
Revolvers

CHAPTER **7**

he very first successful cartridge revolvers were small and
concealable. Smith & Wesson's little Model 1 tip-up was a small-
frame gun in .22 caliber, but it took the pre-Civil War handgun scene
by storm. A trim little revolver, the gun became an instant best seller
simply because if was easy to hide and (mostly) because it fired that
innovative new self-contained metallic cartridge. The latter
advantage was considerable, but it is the norm today. The
concealable nature of those early revolvers made them a frequent
choice for Civil War soldiers who wanted something to drop into the
deep pockets of the heavy wool uniforms used in that day. We don't
wear such massive garments today, but the small revolver remains a
top choice in a concealed carry firearm. Indeed, for many and
possibly *most* applications, it is the best choice. This is a powerful
statement that requires justification.

As we have discussed earlier, the ideal concealed carry handgun
is one that is adequate in the power sense, as well as being small
and light enough to carry habitually. That means sufficiently low
gun mass and weight to preclude any inclination to rationalize
away the need to carry the firearm. And, like any defensive firearm,
it must be quick to get into action and easy to use. A small revolver
fills every one of those criteria extremely well. With a recent change
in the means of construction of small revolvers, we can now buy
the most compact and carryable ones in .357 Magnum, one of the
better defensive cartridges. We are no longer limited to .38 Special
and .38 Special +P.

It should be obvious that an ultra-light .357 Magnum may
present a shooting problem in the sense of severe recoil. The gun
makers are certainly aware of that fact and they continue to make
small steel .357s that are somewhat easier to shoot, but arguably a
little harder to carry. Regardless of the size and weight envelopes,

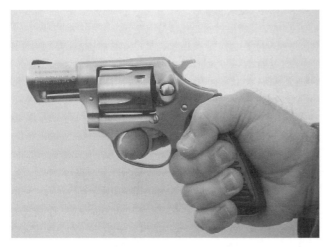

Ruger SP101s come in several calibers, but all are based on the same stainless-steel frame. It is a solid handful of little revolver.

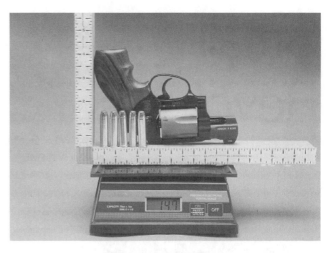

This little internal hammer DAO from Smith & Wesson is based on the Centennial version of the J-frame. A .357 Magnum, it weighs a feathery 14.7 ounces, loaded.

All-steel guns are much easier to shoot and Ruger is well aware of it. There is no light version of the SP101 in any of the calibers. This .357 weighs 28.1 ounces.

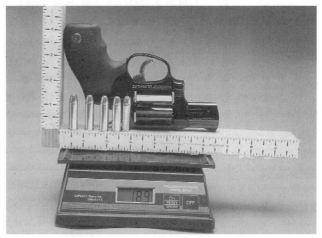

Taurus makes their snubbies in a variety of materials—blue and stainless steel, aluminum alloy, and even titanium. This aluminum M85 weighs 18.9 ounces.

small revolvers are not only among the easiest guns to conceal, but also the quickest guns to get out and working. There are several factors that make this true.

Concealability is a function of size and shape. Depending on how you carry your hideout gun, you may find that the irregular shape of a revolver attracts less attention than an automatic pistol, where the straight lines of slide and receiver print through many kinds of clothing. The slim, rounded butt of a revolver often makes the gun a little easier to recover from a deep pocket of a winter coat or parka. Small revolvers with a

spurred hammer may need to have that spur either reduced or completely removed. Good defensive shooting technique with a revolver is almost invariably through the gun's smooth double-action trigger system. In almost all forseeable defensive scenarios, the ability to manually cock that hammer is not needed. If you effectively "carry bevel" the entire revolver by rounding off corners and edges that the manufacturer didn't, you will have an easy-to-draw, quick-to-shoot little gun. As appealing as these little revolvers certainly are, it's surprisingly that so few makers are still actively developing

There are three major handgun makers currently selling five-shot snubbies in .38 Special and some in .357 Magnum—Ruger, S&W, and Taurus. Rossi and Charter Arms also make some guns in this class.

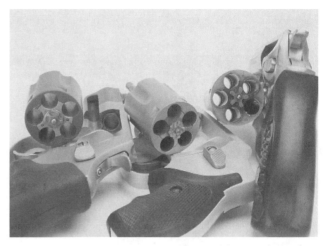

Small five-guns (left to right) from Taurus, Smith & Wesson, and Ruger. Because of the different weights of assorted materials, the guns vary in weight and shootability.

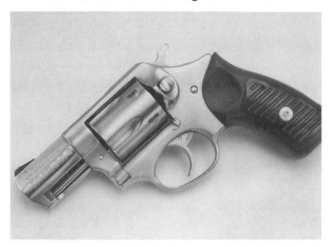

Ruger's little SP101 comes in three adequate defensive calibers. You can have a 9mm, .38 Special (including +P ammo), or a .357 Magnum.

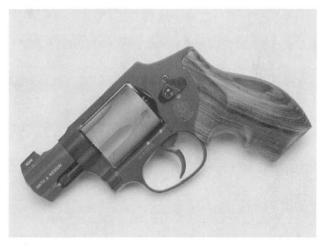

A recent addition to S&W's line of small revolvers is this Model 340PD, which is a scandium frame, titanium cylinder Centennial in .357 Magnum.

and producing them. At present, there are only three makers of truly competitive small revolvers—Ruger, S&W, and Taurus.

Ruger confines itself to a single revolver in several calibers, S&W has a great many variations on the five-shooter theme, and Taurus is aggressively competitive with a good range of products. All are five-shot revolvers with cylinders that swing out to the left for loading and unloading. They all are fairly small and compact, with one kind or another of small grip section. All have fixed sights and it's good to note that the makers all seem to realize that there has to be

enough sight for the shooter to see or the gun will not be accepted. At one time, everyone wanted to install tiny sights on their little guns. Happily enough, those days are gone. Let's look them over.

Sturm, Ruger & Co. introduced the SP101 revolver in 1988. Initially, it was offered only as a .38 Special, specifically engineered for the hot new "+P" loadings of the old cartridge. SP101s are completely new guns and are not based on or developed from earlier models. This was Bill Ruger's first attempt at a little centerfire revolver and he wanted to get it right. He must surely have done so, since I can see no material change

Although they were discontinued for a few years, the internal hammer Centennial revolvers have been big sellers for S&W since their reintroduction in the late 1990s.

Using scandium alloyed with aluminum allows S&W to build an ultra-light frame and yoke that will withstand the pounding of full-power .357 Magnum ammunition.

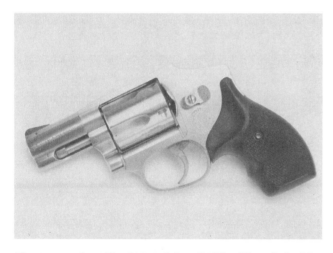

If you can handle the weight, S&W still makes this all stainless-steel Centennial for .357 users. It's called the Model 640.

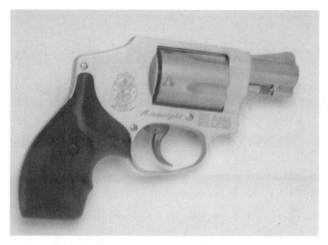

The squared, sort of humpbacked shape of the Centennial makes it very easy to access from pockets or from concealment holsters.

between the 1988 versions and the ones currently on dealer's shelves.

The SP101 frame is investment cast from stainless steel and it uses a rugged new system to lock the cylinder to the frame. All Ruger DA/SA revolvers have a cylinder latch that rocks inwards to open the cylinder for loading or unloading. It is better than the ones used by other makers in that it is completely out of the way in the recoil shield area of the frame. SP101s are extremely strong guns that take a serious amount of abuse. Since the company introduced the first .38s, they have added two other suitable defensive calibers,

.357 Magnum and 9mm Luger. It goes without saying that the .357 Magnum would get the job done. The 9mm Luger doesn't have a Magnum level of power, but when you shoot 9mm loads against .38s using bullets of equivalent weight, the 9mm usually edges the .38 by a small margin of speed. This may be hard to believe in view of the obviously greater case capacity of the .38 Special, but it is true. Of all the rugged and reliable SP101s, I would have to choose the .357 because, like all .357 revolvers, it is also a *de facto* .38 Special.

As previously noted, **Smith & Wesson** has

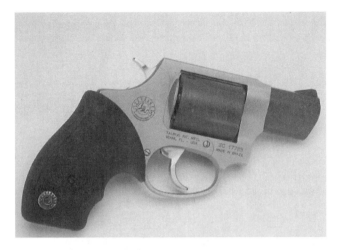

Taurus offers a big array of small revolvers. This little hammer gun is called the Model 85 Multi-Alloy. It will handle any kind of .38 Special ammo.

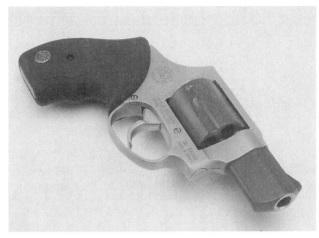

Called the Police model, this Taurus M85 is the multi-alloy type, but comes with the hammer factory-bobbed for ease of use.

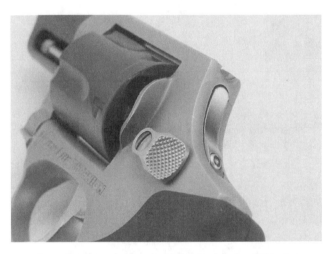

Cutting the hammer away as shown in this photo produces a handgun that is far less likely to snag on the draw than the guns with sharp spurs intact.

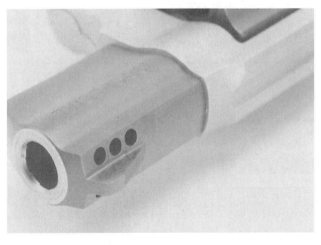

Taurus also fits most of their guns with porting at the muzzle. The holes vent gas upward and somewhat retard muzzle flip.

been making small revolvers since before the Civil War. At the present time, all of their small revolvers originate in one of three variations of the so-called J-frame. The variations are each visibly different and each offers the user a different form of manipulation. The first of these is the Chiefs Special variation and it is the more conventional one. Chiefs Specials all have conventional hammers with checkered spurs and DA/SA lockwork, where the user may either pull the trigger through a long, dynamic arc or cock the hammer with the thumb and press the trigger for a light, crisp release. The same options are available to the user of the second J-frame style, which is called the Bodyguard. It's exactly the same as the Chiefs Special, except for the shape of the frame, which includes a rounded upward extension that almost completely covers the sides of the hammer. Only the tip of the hammer is exposed to allow the shooter's thumb to reach it and cock the hammer if that is needed. The design of this gun assumes that the shooter will infrequently need to cock his hammer, but the rounded, extended frame gives him considerable protection against snagging the hammer spur on the draw.

A blue steel Taurus in use. The little Taurus .38s are favorably priced and come with many options.

The third variation is the Centennial, originally introduced in 1952 and named for the 100th anniversary of the first partnership of Horace Smith and Daniel Wesson. This one is a DAO. There's no way to cock the hammer of a Centennial, because the hammer has no spur and no single-action notch, plus it is completely enclosed within the frame of the gun. S&W's Centennials have a distinct and recognizable humped shape to the rear of their receivers. The action of the revolver is almost sealed from dirt. Further, the contours of the gun are such that there's almost zero possibility of the gun catching on anything.

All three of these guns sell briskly for S&W, so they are offered in weight and finish variations. All three guns are made in stainless steel. The Chiefs Special is called the Model 60, the Bodyguard is a Model 649, and the stainless Centennial is the Model 640. Stainless steel makes these three a bit heavy, but it also makes them more comfortable to shoot with .357 Magnum ammunition. If the shooter needs a lighter gun, Smith & Wesson can give him the same power level in a revolver that is half the weight. The company's line of AirLite revolvers has been developing at a great rate of speed in the past few years. Airweight S&W Js have been offered for many years; they have aluminum alloy frames and steel barrels and cylinders. AirLite Ti revolvers in centerfire calibers were introduced in 1998. They had the same alloy frames, but most of the formerly steel parts (particularly the heavy cylinder) are now Titanium. That is a metal with greater strength than steel, but one that is almost as light as aluminum. The Airweight Centennial weighs 14.5 ounces, but the AirLite version is only 12. As desirable as these little guns certainly were, they were still tied to the pressure levels of the .38 Special +P ammunition.

In 2000, S&W made a technological breakthrough of considerable magnitude. They introduced several new guns in the AirLite series. Instead of being designated the AirLite Ti, the new ones are called AirLite Sc, where the Sc stands for scandium. Scandium is a rare and expensive metal that alloys beautifully with aluminum. It makes a tough, shock-resistant metal that's perfect for building baseball bats, mountain bikes, and lightweight revolver frames capable of taking the shock of firing .357 Magnum ammo. For our discussion here, there are two guns to look at—the Model 360 AirLite Sc and Model 340 AirLite Sc. Both revolvers are .357 Magnums and both weigh just about the same as their Ti brothers. While a steel Model 60 .357 weighs about 23 ounces, its AirLite Sc stablemate weighs 12, or nearly half as much. Their recoil is severe, but never before has there been such power in such a small and light package. Some of the AirLite Ti models will no doubt remain in the S&W catalog, but the lightweight S&W revolvers of tomorrow will have scandium alloy frames.

Being light is very important in today's concealed-carry market and **Taurus International** also produces a series of highly competitive lightweight revolvers on small, five-shot frames. The company's revolvers bear an external resemblance to the products of Smith & Wesson, but they evolved over a period of better than 50 years from a number of different European designs. The guns are made in Brazil in a modern plant and are imported into the Unites States by Taurus International of Miami, Florida.

Where small revolvers are concerned, Taurus absolutely bedazzles the buyer with variety. The basic gun is the Model 85, which has been in production for about a dozen years. The 85s are five-shot .38 Specials that come in many variations, all of which will fire the hot +P variety of .38 Special ammunition. The basic Model 85 action underwent revision for increased smoothness in the past few years, as did all other

Taurus DA/SA or DAO revolvers. The 85 comes in both carbon steel and stainless steel, and they may be purchased with a high polish or matte finish. Steel is a heavy material and these little two-inchers weigh about 21 ounces.

For the fan of the lightweight revolvers, Taurus offers the Model 85 with an aluminum frame and steel barrel/cylinder, which runs to about 17 ounces. But the big breakthrough for Taurus came with their recent introduction of Total Titanium five-shot .38s. All but the barrel liner and certain pins and screws are made of Titanium, which Taurus finishes in a variety of tasteful colors. A so-called "Total Titanium" Taurus in Model 85 format weighs about 15 ounces. Remember that titanium is stronger than steel, but heavier (slightly) than aluminum. To get maximum weight reduction, the Brazilian designers combined the two materials in a so-called "Ultra-Lite" Police Model, which weighs just 13 ounces. It's a bobbed-hammer DAO with an aluminum frame, a titanium cylinder and barrel shroud but a steel barrel liner. And if all of these five-shooters weren't enough, There's a slightly larger gun called the Model 605, which is a stainless steel .357 Magnum with five-shot cylinder capacity. The Taurus catalog is absolutely jammed with variations on the small revolver theme, and we will be looking at some more Taurus revolvers when we get to the medium and large revolvers.

The best of the small revolvers make near ideal carry guns. Some of them might take a bit of judicious carry beveling, but they're all small enough to pack regularly. Breakthrough technology by Smith & Wesson and Taurus means a wide array of weight options. Indeed, one of the lightest defense guns discussed in this book is also one of the more powerful—S&W's scandium J-frame .357.

Medium
Autos

CHAPTER **8**

There are many choices in the field of medium-sized autos. As a matter of fact, it is in this area that most of the automatic pistol makers have focused their greatest attention. For purposes of classification, the medium auto is one that is fairly compact but has a barrel around 4 inches in length. Mediums usually conceal rather easily but are big enough to house decent capacity magazines, particularly in 9mm. The medium auto enjoys a certain amount of popularity, even among uniformed police officers who carry their guns in open holsters.

Within the general field of medium autos, you can find every kind of operating system and every possible variation of triggers and lockwork. Some of these pistols have single-column magazines and others use the doublewide variety. Polymer is a favorite form of receiver construction, but many of the mediums use various aluminum alloys and steel. But best of all, it is possible to find a medium auto in almost every one of the many calibers deemed adequate for personal defense. That runs the gamut from 9mm Luger to .45 ACP.

If you can accept the inevitability of compromise in a tool intended to save your life, the medium auto comes to the fore. As much as we all might like to have a larger and more powerful handgun with a greater capacity on the dark day when it's time to shoot for real, we compromise. We accept something a little smaller with a little less capacity, simply because it is a little more likely to be there when the day we never wanted actually arrives. Viewed in this light, the medium auto is one of the best choices, as long as the handgunner makes a firm commitment to habitually carry the gun. Since we have been over this line of reasoning in several other places in this book, we'll just drop it now and go on to a long series of top-notch defensive autos.

Medium-sized pistols are such guns as the Sig P229 shown here. Aluminum frames keep the fully loaded gun weight in the mid-30-ounce range.

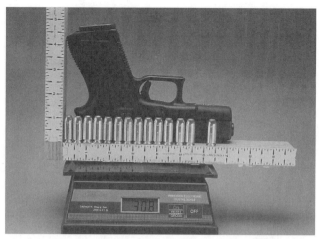

Glock pistols went from zero to near cult status in a matter of just a few years. This is the medium-sized gun in .40 S&W. Fully loaded (13+1), the G23 weighs 30.8 ounces.

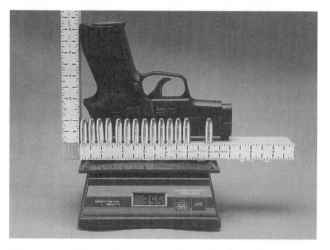

Sigarms pistols are known for their accuracy and user-friendliness. The chunky little P228 is a 13+1 9mm that tips the scales at 35.5 ounces, fully loaded.

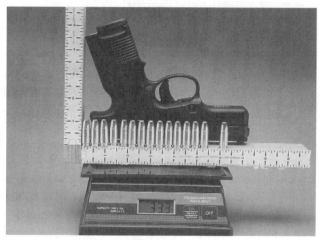

New on the defensive handgun scene we have the Austrian Steyr M pistol. A polymer frame DAO, the gun weighs 33.3 ounces with a full load of cartridges.

Beretta U.S.A. offers an extensive line of fine firearms for sportsmen. In recent years that lineup has grown to include some good handguns. Many of them are derived from the Model 92, which has the distinction of being the official U.S. service pistol as the M9. Only two 92 (9mm) or 96 (.40 S&W) variations fall into the medium category. One is the Centurion, which has a barrel shortened to about 4.3 inches. The other is the Compact, which uses the short Centurion barrel and slide, but also has a butt that's shorter by about an inch. One Compact

variation has a single column magazine to somewhat reduce the gun's girth. If you really want a smaller Beretta for concealed carry, look at the Cougar series. Made in 9mm, .40 S&W, and .45 ACP, the Cougars are completely different pistols with a unique rotating barrel locking system. The lockwork is typical Beretta, which is traditionally very smooth. On many Beretta models, you get a choice of traditional DA/SA with slide-mounted decocker/safety, DAO with a slick slide, or DA/SA with a slide-mounted decocker that has no safety function. Only one

CZ pistols come from the Czech Republic and enjoy a good reputation. This gun is a CZ75 Compact in soft nickel finish. CZs are often carried in the "cocked-and-locked" mode.

Glock makes mediums in several calibers. They include 9mms, .357 Sigs, .40 S&Ws, and even the brand new G36 in .45 ACP.

Heckler & Koch offers the USP pistol in popular calibers. One such gun is the Compact Model in 9mm and .40 S&W.

USPs have lockwork that's easy for a qualified armorer to change to many different styles—DAO (with or without a safety), TDA, decocker/no safety, CZ like, etc. These two pistols have Variant 1 and Variant 2 lockwork.

other maker I can think of offers such an unusual set of options. Beretta also gives you a great many choices in grips and finishes.

Colt Firearms is in an unusual position as this is written. The grand old company is in the midst of problems and their staff and production capacity have been sharply cut back. As far as I can tell, a few handguns are coming out of the Hartford factory every month and some of them are medium autos. The Government Model pistol is the design basis for the Concealed Carry Officer's ACP. Built around the older Officer's Model receiver and the Commander (4 1/4-inch)

slide/barrel unit, the CCO is the best of both worlds. It has a butt that's short enough to readily hide, but long enough to take an aftermarket seven-round magazine. And yes, it is a .45.

CZ U.S.A. is the newly appointed importer of handguns from the Czech Republic. They offer a wide array of pistols, most of them based on the famous CZ75, a full-sized gun. The company has abbreviated the CZ75 in both slide and butt length, producing the CZ75 Compact in 9mm. CZs have an unusual DA/SA trigger system; there is no control provided to decock the hammer for carrying. Most American shooters simply treat the gun as though

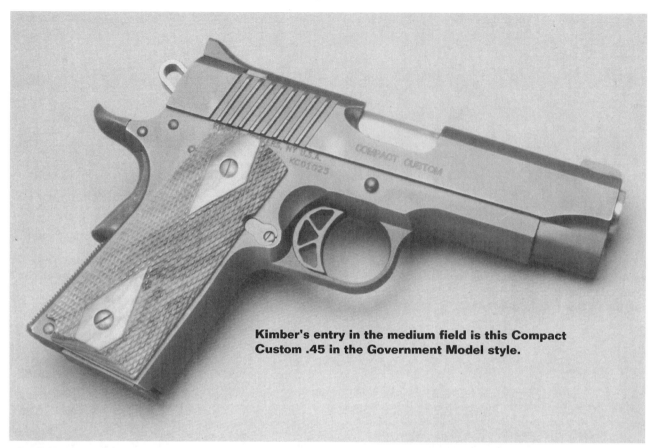

Kimber's entry in the medium field is this Compact Custom .45 in the Government Model style.

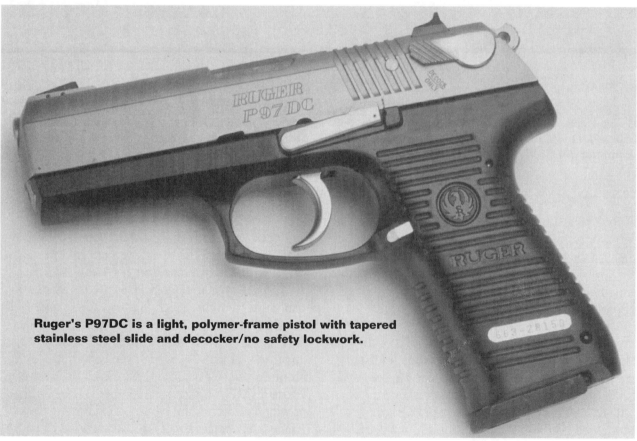

Ruger's P97DC is a light, polymer-frame pistol with tapered stainless steel slide and decocker/no safety lockwork.

it was a straight single action and carry it cocked and locked. New in the last few years is the CZ100, a polymer-framed medium auto noted for its excellent ergonomics and DAO lockwork. This one comes in both 9mm and .40 S&W.

European American Armory (EAA) imports pistols from the Tanfoglio Brothers in Italy. Most of them are large autos we'll check out in Chapter 10. They do, however, have a compact version of their basic Witness pistol. This is a DA/SA service auto inspired by the famous CZ75 design. EAA also has the same gun with a molded polymer receiver. It is called the Witness-P Compact. Witnesses may be had in all of the popular pistol cartridges, including 10mm Auto.

Glock has a pistol for virtually every conceivable need and that includes several mediums. When they introduced their abbreviated version of the original G17 and called it the G19, the gun was very well received. The Glock line has since broadened to include G19 lookalikes in .40 S&W (G23) and .357 Sig (G32). They also have slightly different mediums in 10mm (G29) and .45 ACP (G30). Every Glock works on the basis of the unique Safe Action trigger system, where the moving slide partially loads the striker, leaving a light, almost SA, trigger pull for every shot. By simple substitution of internal parts, a shooter can vary the weight of his Glock trigger pull from 3 1/2 to as much as 12 pounds. It is a versatile and popular pistol, but some shooters bitched for a gun that had a somewhat less bulky butt section. The answer came along just last year in the form of the G36. This one is a medium-sized, single-column, 6+1 .45 that fits my hand better than any other Glock in the series.

Heckler & Koch enjoys a reputation for innovation in firearms. That's true of both design and the means of carrying them out. They were the first to build a polymer and sheet-steel pistol, the first to tie a gas-delayed blowback to high-intensity pistol cartridges and the first to come up with a system of lockwork that should satisfy just about everyone. The latter system is the key to their USP (Universal Service Pistol) series of automatic pistols. In the medium size, H&K offers .45 ACP and 9mm/.40 S&W USPs. They are square and blocky guns that have lockwork unlike any other auto. Armorer or factory substitution of parts can change the USP from DAO to 1911-like

SA or several variants of the DA/SA. In every case the operating lever is on the frame, right under the shooter's thumb. Literally, you can have a USP set up any way your heart desires and either right- or left-handed to boot.

Kimber is a relatively new handgun maker that specializes in pistols of the Government Model stripe. They also make some gorgeous rifles, but their defensive pistol output is pure 1911. We have already looked at the company's small auto, but they also make a medium .45 that's worth your attention. It's the marriage of a short receiver to a special 4-inch barrel and slide. Much like a Colt CCO, but a trifle shorter, the Kimber Compact and Compact Aluminum are steel- and alloy-frame 7+1 .45s that are a very efficient size for carrying. The company maintains an extensive custom shop that will take the basic pistol and upgrade it into a so-called "CDP" (Custom Defense Pistol) that will save you the cost of tuning that all entry-level 1911 pistols seem to need.

Para-Ordnance is a company that pioneered the idea of a high-capacity, double-column .45 magazine. Over the past decade, the company has introduced a growing assortment of 1911-style pistols with this popular feature. They have also come up with a unique DAO trigger system (called the LDA for light double action) that is selling very well as this book is written. Where medium autos are concerned, their best bet is the Para-Ordnance P12, an 11+1 .45 that comes with a shortened butt and barrel. The company has also announced that the P12 will be available in an LDA version. "Paras" have grown to be very popular guns and one of the reasons is that the company still has quantities of pre-ban high-capacity magazines, which were the original reason the guns caught on so strongly.

Sturm, Ruger & Co. started making centerfire automatic pistols within the past 15 years and their lineup has grown quickly. Ruger makes their guns in several sizes and with three completely different styles of lockwork—DA/SA with decocker/safety, DAO, and DA/SA with decocker/no safety. In medium autos, Ruger has the P93 series in 9mm with barrels just under the 4-inch mark and the P95s, which are the same size but lighter by about 4 ounces due to a molded polymer frame. The special lockwork arrangement of these guns produces a very safe handgun that

Sigarms sells lots of these P229s in 9mm. .40 S&W, and the hot cartridge they developed, the .357 Sig. It is an appealing package.

Smith & Wesson probably makes more styles of automatic pistols than anyone else does. This gun is a top-of-the-line Model 3913TSW, a single-column 9mm.

Another good S&W is the single-column Model 4516. A .45 pistol, the gun comes with S&W's original TDA lockwork.

Here is a Springfield Champion in .45 ACP. This is a gun that is essentially the same size as Colt's Commander. Savvy handgunners pack them with the hammer cocked and the safety on.

also has an exceptionally good trigger pull right out of the box. Ruger autos are among the most accurate box-stock pistols currently sold.

Sigarms makes pistols in several sizes and several fall into the medium category. The single-column 9mm P225 has been discontinued, but the P228 that replaced it is an arguably better gun. It has a doublewide magazine of 12 shots (10 for civilians) and a compact and concealable shape. When the .40 S&W cartridge hit the market, Sigarms spent some time carefully developing a pistol to take it. The result was the P229, essentially the same gun as the P228, but fitted

with a milled steel slide to take the sharper bump of the Forty. That gun was perfect for the .357 Sig cartridge, which the company developed in consort with Federal Cartridge. Sig offers no choices in lockwork arrangements and feels there is no need for any. Their newest model is one eagerly awaited for a long time—a medium 6+1 .45 ACP called the P245.

Smith & Wesson makes a huge variety of handguns and a number of them are medium autos. The company's established Third Generation autos of the late 1980s have evolved into the high end "TSW" (Tactical Smith &

Glock's Model 23 pretty well defines the medium auto.

Steyr's M-series pistols have ergonomics that complement the point-shooting systems that are coming back into vogue. They're made for common medium rounds—9mm, .40 S&W, and .357 Sig.

Wesson) pistols of today. These guns are optimized for defensive shooting, with what S&W calls TDA (Traditional Double Action) lockwork with a slide-mounted combination safety and decocker. In medium size, the TSWs include the 9mm Model 3913, .40 S&W Model 4013 and .45 ACP Model 4513. For those who like the DAO variant lockwork, there are the Models 3953, 4053, and 4553. There is also a short series of simplified pistols with TDA lockwork and a "Valueline" moniker. Medium Valuelines include the Model 908 in 9mm and 457 in .45 ACP. There is one final medium auto

from S&W that is a Third Generation variant with TDA lockwork. It is the little 3913LS (for LadySmith). This one has a racy and distinctive frame shape that is popular with both male and female shooters, so much so that it was once made without the LadySmith logo.

Steyr of Austria has made many kinds of automatic pistols throughout the 20th century and their newest ones were recently introduced to the U.S. market. A completely new design, the Steyr M- and S-Series guns follow the trend to polymer receivers, conventional Browning tilt-barrel lockups, and innovative trigger systems. Both M- and S-Series guns are available in 9mm, 40 S&W, and .357 Sig. Although the M-Series pistols are larger than the S-Series, both fall into the medium category. All Steyrs have a very short form of DAO lockwork and unique safety systems. Their most controversial (love it or hate it) feature is ergonomic. The guns have a steeply raked butt section and a shape that raises the hand to a location very close to the axis of the bore. Particularly in 9mm, Steyrs handle very well, with very little felt recoil or muzzle flip. There is an administrative safety that works on a key lock to secure the pistol (loaded) when not in use.

Taurus International is well represented in both pistol and revolver categories. Not surprisingly, they have several autos that are in the medium category. When Taurus introduced the first of these guns several years ago, their main products had some external resemblance to the products of Beretta and S&W. Their medium autos do not and the fact that Taurus was initiating their own designs was a bit of a surprise. The pistols are closed-slide, locked-breech design with a Browning-type tilting barrel lockup. Made in 9mm, .357 Sig, and .40 S&W, the Taurus mediums have doublewide magazines and one of the better trigger systems of them all. On the Taurus frame, there are a pair of levers (one on each side) that serve to put the gun on safe when up and ready it for shooting when down. But the shooter can also push the lever even farther down to decock the hammer if it happens to be cocked. This gives the Taurus Models PT911, PT940, and PT957 remarkable tactical flexibility.

Vektor is a new name on the American handgun scene, but the South African company's designs are innovative in the extreme. They make a series of large pistols we'll get to in Chapter 10, but their medium deserves a close look here. Called the CP1, this is a 9mm pistol with a gas-delayed blowback operating system. It works on the basis of a gas cylinder in the dust cover area. A piston in the cylinder is attached to the front nose of the slide in such a way that gas pressure on the tip of the piston tends to hold the slide closed until gas pressure drops. It works in a fashion somewhat like the H&K P7 and Heritage Stealth. But the gun's wildly futuristic contours are probably a more attention-grabbing feature. The CP1 looks like a pistol from a Buck Rogers comic strip. There are virtually no edges or corners of any kind, making this a pistol that will tuck away in a great variety of positions around a shooter's gear or person. It's a DAO. The variant CP2 in .40 S&W has a tilting barrel locking system and a pivoting trigger. Either gun is a great choice from a concealment point of view.

As you can see, there are many options in medium autos. Most of them tend to be in 9mm or .40 S&W and most have some form of DA/SA or DAO trigger system. There are a few .45s available and even some 10mms and .357 Sigs. Nothing listed in this chapter is a bad choice; it really comes down to what caliber and system you like and how well a particular gun with those features fits your hand and generally works for you. For sure, it's buyer's choice.

Medium
Revolvers

hen the shooter who likes the revolver for a concealed-carry firearm steps up to a medium-sized gun, he increases his options quite a bit. Probably the most significant area of greater choice is in caliber. All of the little revolvers we discussed earlier share the same .355- to .357-inch bore size. They're 9mms, .38 Specials, or .357 Magnums. By going to a little larger frame we can manage to squeeze in some larger calibers—.41 Magnum, .44 Special, and even the legendary .45 Colt. If you refer back to Chapter 3, you'll recall how important the size of the bullet hole actually is. While modern ammunition manages to expand with great reliability, it is always better to begin with a bullet that's big before it ever exits the muzzle of your handgun. The medium revolver is an excellent way to deliver heavy bullets in sizes up to .45 caliber.

Naturally, the guns are a little larger and heavier. Compared to the small revolvers, the mediums may be of such a size that they're far from ideal for a few shooters in some concealment situations. But a majority of shooters find a carefully selected medium revolver to be fairly concealable. Aside from the possibility of a larger bore and heavier bullets, the mediums are in a size and weight bracket to deliver another shot or two. For many years, the medium revolver, usually a S&W K-frame or Colt Official Police size, was the most common police service six-shooter. Both companies made the guns with a variety of different barrel lengths—2 through 6 inches in length. For purposes of discussion, we'll confine ourselves to guns with barrels no longer than 3 inches. They're generally built on true medium frames, although there are a couple of 3-inch small revolvers that are too long to be considered in the small revolver chapter.

There's also a new size of revolver frame that falls between the true medium and the large revolver frames. S&W really began this trend with their so-called L-frame revolvers. Their smaller K-frames

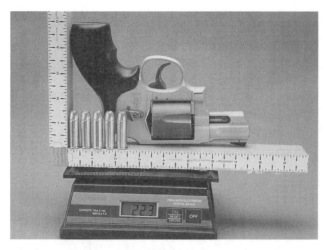

With five rounds of Winchester 200-grain Silvertips, the S&W Ti Model 296 weighs a feathery light 22.3 ounces. The frame is aluminum alloy.

Taurus, the hard-charging Brazilian handgun maker, has a number of competitive revolvers in the medium category. This is a Total Titanium .44 Special.

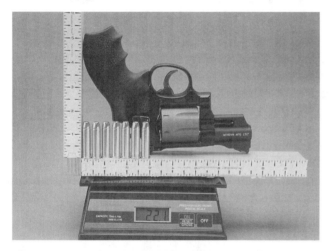

The newest thing from S&W is the scandium revolver. Using the light metal with aluminum in the frame allows them to build a seven-shot .357 Magnum weighing 22.1 ounces loaded.

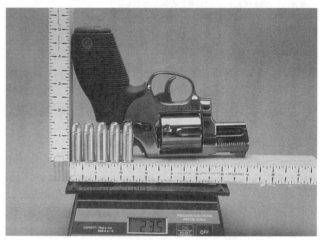

Titanium is lighter than steel, but just as strong. That lets Taurus build this five-shot .44 Special that weighs 23.5 ounces.

were entirely adequate for the type of ammunition used at the time of their introduction in the mid-1950s. But when the market demanded a hotter, higher-velocity type of ammunition, Smith & Wesson noticed an increased frequency of damage to their K-frame magnums. They responded with a slightly larger revolver that accepts a diverse array of hotter ammo—the L-frame. When other makers came along with their updated and modernized guns, they were close to the S&W product in size and weight. When fitted with a 2-, 2 1/2-, or 3-inch barrel, one of these medium or light heavyweight frames makes a decisive

concealed-carry revolver. They have the same advantages as any revolver. They're simple to manage and quick into action. Out of the box, their triggers are very good and the brief attention of a good revolversmith can make them excellent.

Revolvers are archaic mechanisms in the grand design, but they are nonetheless accurate beyond the demands of defensive shooting. The better of the modern ones are extremely accurate, which is a confidence builder if not an essential element of a short-range defensive revolver. Revolvers were once criticized as slow to reload, but speed loaders and moon clips have somewhat

Although this little J-frame S&W is only a five-round gun, the longer and heavier barrel puts it in medium category. The gun is 3-inch .357 Magnum.

For years, S&W's K-frame revolvers were the dominant guns in the medium category. In .38 Special/.357 Magnum, they were the most common revolver.

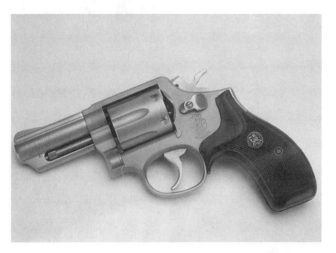

This is a LadySmith variation of the Model 65 revolver. It's a six-shot .357 Magnum revolver on a medium frame. A little heavy, but a great shooter.

Smith & Wesson uses its medium-heavy L-frame for many things. This heavy-barreled revolver is an all-steel .44 Special called the Model 696.

softened the edge of that criticism. And there is one final advantage of a medium revolver.

Medium revolvers all come with small, rounded grip frames. The various factories provide grip panels to go on the frame. If what the manufacturer provides is not sufficient for your needs, there are dozens of aftermarket grip makers who produce a considerable array of grips of many sizes and shapes. Made of wood, rubber, plastic, stag, and other materials, these grips give the medium revolver a considerable advantage. It is possible to fit a pair of stocks that work for the small-handed shooter who needs a small grip on his gun.

The mediums offer many advantages, the greatest of which is probably the simplicity of operation that is the hallmark of all revolvers. For defensive purposes, the single-action trigger pull is seldom used. Most of the time, it will be a smooth sweep of the double-action trigger through a long, dynamic arc. With practice, this is a skill most shooters develop without difficulty. Mediums also deliver a good ratio of power to weight/mass. Their capacity may be a little limited, but high capacity is something that most situations simply don't require. With this preamble, we can now start to look at the various models of medium revolvers.

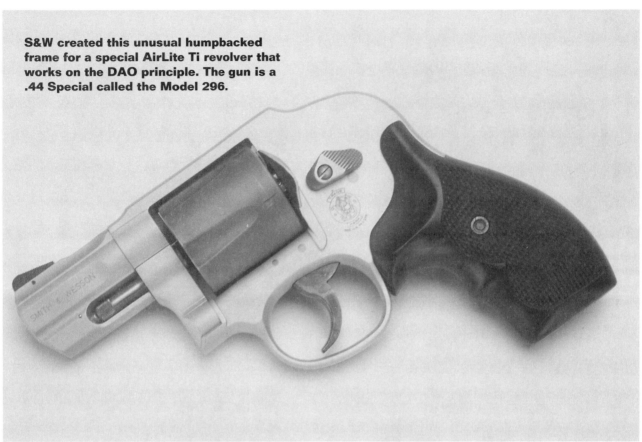

S&W created this unusual humpbacked frame for a special AirLite Ti revolver that works on the DAO principle. The gun is a .44 Special called the Model 296.

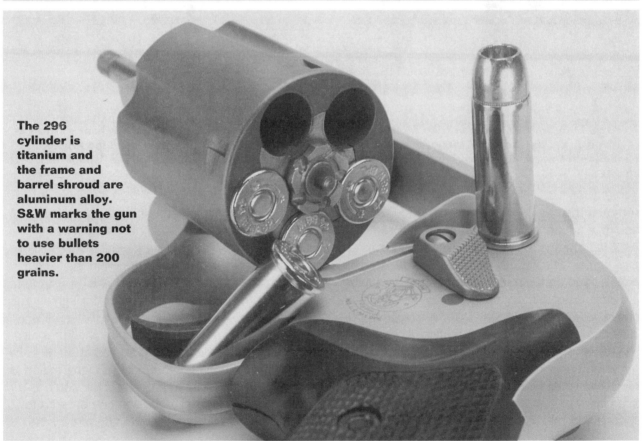

The 296 cylinder is titanium and the frame and barrel shroud are aluminum alloy. S&W marks the gun with a warning not to use bullets heavier than 200 grains.

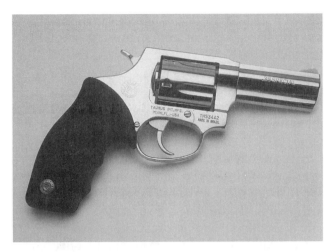

Here's a Taurus five-shot .38 Special with a very pointedly heavy barrel some 3 inches in length. Greater length puts the gun in the medium category.

Taurus uses a high-polish bright blue finish on this 2-inch Total Titanium .44 Special. It is a light and powerful revolver with excellent trigger action.

The first maker is **Sturm, Ruger & Co.,** which is most commonly referred to simply as "Ruger." We have already looked at their SP101 revolver in .38 Special, 9mm, and .357 Magnum. It is a small revolver in the sense of its five-shot cylinder and unobtrusive fixed sights. When you add another inch to the barrel, the SP101 is a little harder to hide and becomes a medium revolver. The factory offers all three defensive calibers in 3 1/16-inch barrels. As strong and durable as the little GP101s certainly are, I would have to consider the 3-inchers to be among the better choices in medium defensive revolvers.

Ruger does provide another option in the medium revolver class. It is the rugged GP100 revolver. For concealed-carry use, the GP100 comes with fixed sights and a 3-inch barrel. Weight runs to either 35 or 36 ounces, depending on the length of the shroud surrounding the ejector rod under the barrel. There's a small price difference between the blue and stainless-steel versions. I particularly like the very nicely shaped round butt grip on this gun. It is well designed for a large variety of hands. Like everything else Bill Ruger ever made, the GP100 is a rugged revolver if there ever was one.

With every passing year, the quality and complexity of the revolver lineup at **Taurus International** grows larger. They currently make revolvers in several frame sizes and there are a great many viable choices for concealed-carry

handgunners. Their latest innovation is Total Titanium revolvers in many sizes, calibers, and colors. Using the wondrous miracle metal that is all the rage these days, Taurus builds a series of snubbie mediums that are about a third lighter than the same guns in steel (which is also still available). There's another advantage to using titanium. The material is corrosion-resistant in the same way that stainless steel defies rust with minimal care.

We have already talked about Taurus' bread 'n' butter Model 85 snubbie, a five-shot .38 Special. Equipped with a 3-inch barrel, the Model 85 falls in the medium revolver category. There are two Model 85 variations with the 3-inch tube, one blue and one stainless. But the Brazilian designers have also come up with a somewhat larger frame and that's the one that gives a completely new meaning to the term medium revolver. On this so-called "compact" frame Taurus designers have produced an entire series of great medium frame short-barreled defensive revolvers. The frame comes in aluminum, titanium, and both carbon and stainless steel.

First consider the Model 817, which has the weight-saving aluminum frame; this one uses a steel cylinder and will take the hottest .38 Special +P loads available. It has a seven-shot cylinder. When you make the same gun entirely from steel, it's called the Model 617 and retains the seven-shot cylinder, but this time, it's seven .357

Magnums. This means you have a strong 2-inch revolver weighing 28.2 ounces that carries seven rounds of one of the more powerful defensive cartridges in existence. The use of this frame for a seven-shot Magnum revolver is fairly new, but it has been in use with another legendary manstopper for several years. The cartridge is the .44 Special, which is experiencing an upsurge in popularity, clearly attributable to guns like this one. Taurus calls their .44 Special the Model 445. There are a number of finish options and even a 20.3-ounce lightweight gun. The 445s are also offered with bobbed hammers in a DAO version and with barrel porting to reduce muzzle rise.

There are a couple of other variations in the Taurus Compact series. You can have the gun in the same .44 Special format (five-shot cylinder, 2-inch barrel), but chambered for the .45 Colt cartridge, with the same lightweight option. That is a powerhouse load that has been getting it done since 1873. And you can also buy essentially the same gun in—believe it or not—.41 Magnum. This one has another half-inch of barrel. But the most interesting of all the guns in this series are the Total Titanium versions. Made almost completely from titanium, these lightweight, corrosion-resistant snubbies are made in almost all of the variations and calibers we have already mentioned. That includes .357 and .41 Magnums, plus .44 Specials and .45 Colts. Always style conscious, the Brazilians offer these revolvers in a choice of colors—gold, gray, and blue. Taurus has a really diverse set of options in defense revolvers.

Smith & Wesson's catalog for 2000 shows a whole bunch of great medium revolvers built with the style and quality that have made the S&W name recognized around the world. Two of them are actually the small J-frames that make it to our medium status when you install the 3-inch barrel. The Model 60 is a .357 Magnum with adjustable sights mounted on the short barrel; the 337 is an AirLite Ti Kit Gun in .38 Special. The next step up in frame size for S&W is the K-frame. This is the foundation for a century of packable six-shot revolvers in .38 Special and later in the 20th century, .357 Magnum. The original Model 10 Military & Police revolver is no longer made in short barrels, but its stainless counterpart, the

Model 64, comes in 2- and 3-inch variations. You can also have a dimensionally similar gun called the Model 65 in .357 Magnum. The Model 66 Combat Magnum comes with a short 2 1/2-inch barrel and adjustable sights.

S&W's L-frame is a slightly larger version of the K-frame and is intended for use with the full range of .357 Magnum ammo. Most of the L-frames are bigger guns than mediums, but both the six-shot Model 686 and seven-shot Model 686 Plus are made with full lugged barrels 2 1/2 inches long. There is also a very interesting gun called the Model 696. It is a stainless-steel 3-incher with fully adjustable sights and a five-shot cylinder chambered for the .44 Special cartridge. At 36 ounces, this is a fairly heavy revolver, but S&W has something special in store for those who like that .44 Special cartridge. It's the Model 296, a humpbacked version of the DAO Centennial built on a special version of the L-frame. This is an AirLite Ti gun with an aluminum alloy frame and a titanium cylinder. It weighs just 18.9 ounces.

You may recall our discussion of the new S&W AirLite Sc guns in the chapter on small revolvers. Scandium is a rare metal that alloys with aluminum to produce a very shock-resistant metal that's ideal for revolver frames. In the medium-frame scandium models, S&W offers two guns—a 3-inch L-frame with a seven-shot titanium cylinder in .357 Magnum, and a tapered-barrel 2 1/2-incher with a matte gray finish and the same seven-shot .357 Magnum cylinder. Both have adjustable sights, which are usually out of place on a concealed carry gun intended for close work. I believe this one will do very well for S&W in both the civilian and law enforcement markets.

Medium revolvers have been around for a long time and show every sign of staying with it for the foreseeable future. As always, it is simplicity of operation that makes them attractive. There are no slides to rack, no safeties to switch, and no magazines to fill. Punch open the cylinder and check the readiness of the gun. Pull the trigger through that long DA arc and it fires. To many shooters, the medium revolver is the only way to go and they are fortunate in that there are more viable choices than ever before.

Large Autos

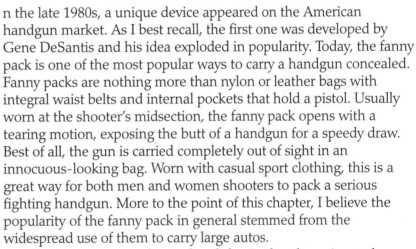

n the late 1980s, a unique device appeared on the American handgun market. As I best recall, the first one was developed by Gene DeSantis and his idea exploded in popularity. Today, the fanny pack is one of the most popular ways to carry a handgun concealed. Fanny packs are nothing more than nylon or leather bags with integral waist belts and internal pockets that hold a pistol. Usually worn at the shooter's midsection, the fanny pack opens with a tearing motion, exposing the butt of a handgun for a speedy draw. Best of all, the gun is carried completely out of sight in an innocuous-looking bag. Worn with casual sport clothing, this is a great way for both men and women shooters to pack a serious fighting handgun. More to the point of this chapter, I believe the popularity of the fanny pack in general stemmed from the widespread use of them to carry large autos.

Virtually everyone who studies defensive handgunning at the established schools at least considers a large auto and many make it their gun of choice. There are so many advantages to the big pistol and such a diverse assortment of them on dealer's shelves that only their size and weight keep them out of a lot more holsters. By our classification system, an automatic pistol with a barrel around 5 inches or less and/or a bulky receiver is a large auto. The guns are produced with a big variety of lockwork, capacity, and caliber options. Many of the big ones are fairly light as a result of polymer or alloy frames. By virtue of their size and weight, large autos require more commitment on the part of the shooter, but if the assault on your person actually comes, the decision to carry a big gun will pay off in spades.

That's because the bulk of a big auto means a useful magazine capacity and a bore size that makes for fight-stopping efficiency. The weight that makes it hard to carry is the same weight that soaks up recoil and facilitates fast pairs. The gun's size may be such that a

One of the most enduring defensive pistols of all time is the Colt Government Model. This is the Commander version, made with a steel frame for greater shootability.

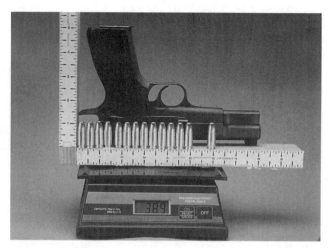

John Browning started design work on the pistol that became a classic and the first to use a high-capacity magazine. The Hi-Power weighs 38.9 ounces fully loaded (13+1).

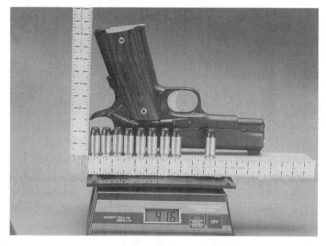

An all-steel Colt Commander is a fairly heavy pistol. Today's magazines hold eight rounds. One more in the chamber raises the weight to a hefty 41.6 ounces.

Beretta's Model 92F is the current U.S. service pistol. The gun is called the M9 in service jargon. A very smooth-operating pistol, the big Beretta has a 15+1 capacity.

presentation from concealment is a dab slow, but the size also means a longer barrel and sight radius—and a far more pointable pistol. Virtually every characteristic of a large auto favors choosing it as a fighting handgun, except the size and weight difficulties associated with carrying it to the fight. For many concealed-carry permit holders, the need for compromise on something else gets forced on them.

At this point in the book, we need to take a look at the range of choices available in the large auto. As we have done in other chapters, let's take it alphabetically and begin with **Beretta U.S.A.** As

most shooters are aware, Beretta makes the current U.S. service auto, which is called the M9. Beretta makes that same pistol in civilian trim and calls it the Model 92FS. This is a rather large pistol with a long slide and barrel. It also has a rather thick, bulky butt section. Beretta 92s are 9mms, but the pistol is also made as the M96 in .40 S&W. There are plenty of finish options and even some special edition guns with competition sights and slides contoured for durability. Best of all, the gun comes with three distinct lockwork variations. The FS versions are DA/SA with a slide-mounted decocker/safety and the D series are DAOs with

Browning had to make some modifications to get the Hi-Power beefed up to take the new .40 S&W cartridge. The resulting pistol is 2 1/2 ounces heavier than the 9mm version.

Arguably the king of fighting handguns, the big Colt has ruled the roost for almost a century. It is a strong and reliable handgun.

A few CZ75s made their way into the country in the late '70s and started a craze that leveled off in the early 1990s. An advanced pistol, the big CZs demand a large hand.

CZ currently makes a big .45 pistol called the CZ97. The gun is large and heavy, but would be a good choice for those who can manage the weight.

slick slides and spurless hammers. Arguably the best Berettas are the G models with a slide-mounted decocker—no safety.

The future of one of the best automatic pistols ever built was a little clouded for a while. The gun is the classic P35 or Hi-Power pistol imported by **Browning.** Made in Belguim for 65 years, the 9mm Hi-Power is one of the world's finest pistols. It is a pure SA gun that has the world's first successful high-capacity magazine (13 rounds). Hi-Powers are beautifully machined pistols that enjoy a legendary reputation for reliability. The Belgian designers were able to adapt the basic

pistol to the .40 S&W cartridge by using a modified slide that is 2 1/2 ounces heavier. It is an excellent choice as a concealed-carry gun, but Browning wasn't importing the Hi-Power for a while. I'm pleased to report that the pistols are once again available from Browning.

Two good concealed-carry guns from Colt are the Colt Government Model and the Commander. Both guns are available in the original .45 ACP caliber and .38 Super. The M1911A1 is the yardstick by which all combat pistols are measured and it's being produced at an increasing rate. While it is arguably an archaic mechanism, the

FNMI is an American subsidiary of Belgium's Fabrique Nationale. They make this gun, called the FN49, in both 9mm and .40 S&W. It's a DAO with a polymer frame.

Glock started with a full-sized pistol and currently makes high-capacity autos in several calibers. This is their big Model 21, a 13+1 .45 ACP and a great pistol.

CONCEALED CARRY

Here's the original 9mm G17 Glock compared with the .45 caliber G21. The larger caliber gun is beefier in grip and slide thickness.

H&K's big service pistol is designed in an effort to satisfy the pickiest of American shooters. By substitution of parts, the gun can have any style of lockwork imaginable.

Made in Croatia, the HS 2000 is a very different pistol built on a polymer receiver. As of early 2002, we are advised that Springfield Armory will market the gun.

Kimber makes many variations of the Government Model. This Commander-sized pistol is a .45 called the Pro Eclipse II. Kimbers are great values.

Colt .45 has a large body of doctrine surrounding its use. If the original full-size pistol is too big and heavy for you, consider the shorter and lighter Commander pistol, which comes in both steel and lightweight frame versions. That latter gun is often the choice of professional users. There has never been a firearm so widely copied and modified.

CZ USA imports the excellent CZ75 pistols from the Czech Republic in 9mm and .40 S&W calibers. They also have the CZ85 version of the same gun, which differs mainly in the sense that it has been fitted with both an ambidextrous safety and an unusual ambidextrous slide lock. CZs have

a good reputation, which stems in part from the qualified endorsement of Jeff Cooper. The most recent addition to the Czech lineup is the CZ97, which is a very large, all-steel .45 pistol with typical CZ cocked-and-locked trigger operation that also has an alternative first-shot DA capability.

European American Armory (EAA) is a Florida-based importer of handguns from several European locales. In the large pistol area, they have a number of varieties of their Witness pistol, which is made in Italy by Fratelli Tanfoglio. Tanfoglio pistols come in many calibers and many variations, all of them bearing an unmistakable

Para-Ordnance was the first to make a widebody .45 pistol and still does so. This one is the top-of-the-line Signature series gun, a 14+1 .45 ACP.

Ruger makes P-series autos in the main calibers. This is one of several different guns in their lineup. Ruger autos have very smooth triggers and excellent accuracy.

A pair of Sig guns—the full size P226 and P220. Sig pioneered the decocker/no safety system. Their guns are widely used by American police agencies.

S&W collaborated with Walther of Germany on this very advanced service pistol which is called the SW99. The gun has three different trigger modes.

resemblance to the original CZ pistols. CZs of any kind are popular in Europe and EAA offers variations and calibers that are not to be found elsewhere. They even have polymer-frame Witnesses in colors.

FNMI (Fabrique Nationale Manufacturing Incorporated) is a subsidiary of the legendary Belgian military and sporting arms factory and is located in the United States. They have a police and military type auto in 9mm and .40 S&W. The FN49 has a polymer receiver and machined steel slide. It also has a rather different form of DAO operation that requires a fair amount of conscious

and deliberate effort to fire. That is by design and this pistol is clearly intended to be used by police, military, and civilian shooters as a defensive tool. With the right ammunition, the FN49 is a decently accurate combat pistol.

Austria's **Glock** makes the same basic pistol in almost any size and caliber a handgunner could want. Naturally, many of those are large pistols. With the exception of the new medium-sized G36 .45, all Glocks are double-column magazine guns with the company's proprietary Safe Action trigger system. Full-size Glocks come in all calibers (G17 in 9mm; G22 in .40; G31 in .357 Sig; G20 in

Smith & Wesson simplified the Third Generation design and produced the economical Valueline series of pistols. This is a 10-shot .40 S&W called the Model 410.

There are several variations of the original Third Generation pistols. This one is a very smooth DAO 9mm pistol called the Model 5944.

S&W introduced the Sigma line to compete with the Glocks. Sigmas remain a great buy in a high-capacity pistol.

The silhouette of the Browning Hi-Power is instantly recognizable. Since 1935, the pistol has been in continuous production—and in continuous use.

10mm, and G21 in .45 ACP). There are even some special competition-oriented models that have longer than usual slides. Glocks have a strong following of enthusiasts, and with good reason. These are durable, effective pistols that serve with distinction on many police departments nationwide. The enthusiastic acceptance of the big Glocks has produced an unusual side effect; the price of pre-ban high-capacity magazines for the big Glocks has skyrocketed.

Heckler & Koch paid close attention to the demands of the U.S. market when they produced the USP. It is a big gun in 9mm or .40 S&W and a bigger gun yet when they size it up to take .45 ACP cartridges. USPs come with a variety of different styles of lockwork and as a result of that situation, an H&K armorer can configure the very same USP pistol to work in the same manner as almost any modern auto you want to choose from this book. H&K pioneered a number of different features for fighting handguns, including a rail system forward of the trigger guard that accepts a high-intensity white light. This feature is no affectation, particularly for police officers. For civilian concealed carry it probably is bulky enough to be impractical.

Taurus makes this big .45 ACP pistol for the defensive handgun market. The gun comes with a barrel porting system to reduce recoil.

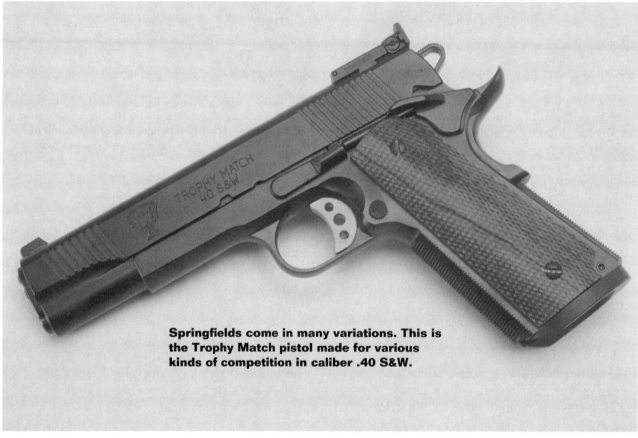

Springfields come in many variations. This is the Trophy Match pistol made for various kinds of competition in caliber .40 S&W.

HS 2000 pistols are made in a small and very modern plant in Croatia. While the design is unique, it incorporates a number of modern features—polymer frame, machined slide, and a simplified form of DAO lockwork. The system uses part of the action of the moving slide to partially load or pre-cock the internal striker. This is somewhat like the system pioneered by Glock in the 1980s. HS 2000s have very shootable ergonomics and an ambidextrous magazine catch. They also use a feature that is seldom seen in a pistol these days—a grip safety that works like the M1911A1's.

Kimber makes Government Model pistols of very high quality. Like my favored GMC trucks, they also sell the basic gun in several trim levels. The Kimber Custom Shop currently tunes up the basic Kimber pistols and sells them as CDP (Custom Defense Package) versions. The price tag runs a little higher, but it is money well spent. One of the better choices in the Kimber line is the (roughly) Commander-size .45 called the Pro Carry. A 26-ounce 8+1 .45 auto is still hard to beat. The Kimber Custom Shop is willing to perform a little customizing or a lot, and at very reasonable prices.

Magnum Research offers a couple of defense pistols worthy of consideration. One is a version of the CZ75 mostly made in Italy by Tanfoglio and finished in Israel. It comes in the short calibers—9mm and .40 S&W—and is called the Baby Eagle. The other gun is a unique but rather heavy .45 pistol called the onePRO. This one has many of the modern features.

Para-Ordnance pioneered the doublewide magazine in .45 pistols and other firms have followed suit. Para still pretty well rules that roost because of the decent quality of their guns and the entirely reasonable price tags on them. You can have a Para-Ordnance pistol of several different sizes, in blue or stainless steel and with alloy or steel frames. Pre '94 Paras came with 14-round magazines in .45 ACP, but they're equipped with 10-rounders now. Para does give you the means of acquiring pre-ban high cap magazines at far less than gunshow prices. The company came out with a special DAO version of the basic P-14 .45. It's called the LDA (Light Double Action) and they also have a "flat" Para with a single-column magazine. The LDA is catching on very well.

Fifteen years ago, there were no centerfire autos from **Ruger**, but times have changed. Ruger has four different 9mm pistols—the P89, P93, P94, and P95—plus two .45s, the P90 and P97. The P94 also comes in .40 S&W and some models have polymer receivers, while others have steel or alloy. Ruger has something for everyone in the lockwork department, with DA/SA decocker/no safety, DAO, and DA/SA safety/decocker mechanisms. While Ruger's pistols tend to be rather blocky, they are also way above the average in accuracy. Ruger's trigger system seems to be one of the safer ones, as well as being one of the smoother ones.

Sigarms builds two large autos. First there is the P220, which comes in .45 ACP and the uncommon .38 Super. Second, there is the P226, which is chambered in .40 S&W, .357 Sig, and 9mm Luger. Most of the P226s have 12- or 15-round magazines and go to the police service. The .45 caliber P220s are widely available and are one of the top choices in a DA/SA automatic pistol. They all have alloy frames and are therefore not onerously heavy to carry. The decocker is well positioned and contributes to a DA/SA lockwork system that has been copied, but never quite equaled.

Smith & Wesson has had the biggest variety of models in almost every category we've looked into and this one is no exception. First, consider the Sigma series of pistols. These were introduced with considerable fanfare several years ago and it was obvious they were intended to compete with Glock. Full-sized service guns with DAO systems and polymer receivers, the Sigmas remain very nice-handling and inexpensive autos. There are also a couple of big autos in the also-inexpensive Valueline series. They are the Model 910 in 9mm and 410 in .40 S&W. More variations are in the TSW series—the 5906s, 4006s, and 4566s. These are top-of-the-line S&Ws that grew out of the original Third Generation guns of a decade back. Finally, there is the SW99 in both 9mm and .40 S&W. This is a joint product of Smith & Wesson and Walther. It is a very advanced service pistol with trigger options like no other gun. It also has several other unique features like interchangeable backstraps to tailor the gun to different hand sizes. This is an excellent pistol.

Springfield makes a large variety of Government Model pistols and they are widely regarded—along with Kimber—as the main competition for Colt's lagging sales. The Springfield lineup includes a 10-shot pistol with doublewide magazine, a couple of smaller guns and a lot of finish and sight options. Springfield maintains an active staff of excellent pistolsmiths in their Custom Shop and they are capable of making many types of improvements on your new Springfield. There is one gun in their catalog that seems to go almost unnoticed. It is a full-sized M1911A1 type pistol with 5-inch barrel and slide, but made with a lightweight receiver. That is unique—and a very good carry gun.

Although **Taurus** seems to be concentrating on small concealed-carry guns and monster revolvers, they are still producing quantities of their Model 92 and 96 series autos. If these guns resemble the M9 service pistol, it's because they had exactly the same origins. That is the Beretta design plant in Italy. Beretta built a plant in Brazil to build their Model 92 service pistol for the Brazilian police and military service. They sold that plant to Taurus, who put it to work making the original Taurus automatic pistols that are dead ringers for Berettas. They are excellent guns that are reasonably priced. Taurus also makes a large .45 auto of their own design.

We have danced rather quickly through an assortment of large defensive automatic pistols. Arguably, they are among the hardest pistols to carry with any degree of comfort and ease. But they are just as arguably the best choice when it comes to really shooting.

Large Revolvers

When the barrel of a revolver grows to more than 4 inches in length, it is a big handgun. It's also hard to conceal in almost all situations. Yeah, I know—we've all seen moviedom's Inspector Harry Callahan draw that 6 1/2-inch .44 Magnum from under his sport coat in the early scenes of *Dirty Harry*. But Clint Eastwood is a very tall man and he didn't have to carry that cannon around for the hours that a real San Francisco PD detective works. The overwhelming majority of us just aren't going to find themselves packing any revolver with a barrel longer than 4 inches, particularly when it is by choice and not as a matter of duty. Don't make the mistake of comparing a revolver with a 4-inch barrel to an automatic pistol with a 4-inch barrel. The revolver is longer and often heavier, simply because of the way we measure barrels in handguns and because of the number of chambers involved.

Customarily, we measure a revolver barrel from the face of the cylinder to the muzzle, which leaves out the length of the chambers in the cylinder. An automatic pistol goes from the breech face to the muzzle, obviously including the chamber. This system doesn't make for a valid comparison, but trying to correct it at this point in history would only further confuse the issue. Also, there are up to eight chambers in a modern large revolver and each of them requires a solid wall of thick steel completely around. In an automatic pistol, it's one firing chamber and it's part of the barrel. Suffice it to say that a large revolver is probably the hardest gun to conceal and may be the toughest to carry on a regular basis. Does this make it the worst possible choice for a concealed carry firearm?

Not necessarily. It's pretty obvious that choosing a defensive handgun is one darned compromise after another, so you have to balance what you get in the way of performance from a large revolver against what you give up in increased packable weight and

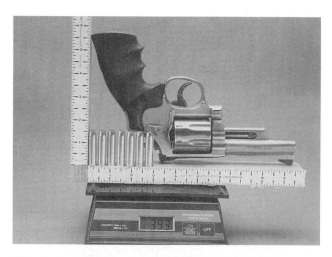

This large revolver is one of S&W's Mountain Guns, so named for their somewhat lighter than usual characteristics. The gun is a seven-shot .357 Magnum.

It is about as long as you can comfortably conceal, but the S&W Model 686+ Mountain Gun is nonetheless an all-steel revolver weighing 39.3 ounces loaded with seven rounds.

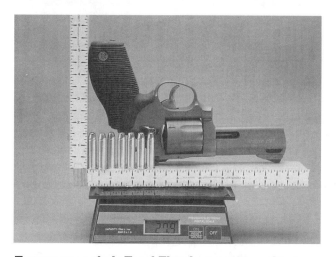

Taurus uses their Total Titanium construction to build this Tracker. It is an adjustable sight, 4-inch, seven-shot .357 Magnum weighing 27.9 ounces loaded.

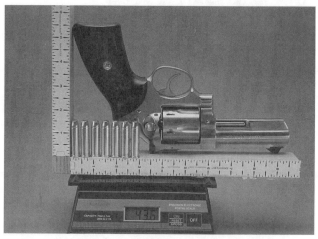

Ruger puts a great deal of stainless steel into their rugged GP100 revolver. That raises the weight to 43.6 ounces, but the gun is very comfortable to shoot.

concealable bulk. Modern large revolvers are made in a series of proven fight-stopping calibers starting with .357 Magnum and working up to .44 Magnum. The latter caliber may be grossly excessive with most loadings, but several makers offer special mid-velocity loads that edge the beloved .44 Special just a little. You don't have to pack your Dirty Harry gun with 300-grain elk loads; there are options.

Using carefully selected ammo, the large revolver becomes a very attractive proposition when the fight actually starts. Most of these guns have enough weight to soak up the recoil of typical defensive ammunition. Obviously, they are sufficiently powerful for the job at hand. Moreover, my machine rest testing has shown me they are exceptionally accurate. I concede that most defensive shootings are close-range affairs, but there are some occasions when accuracy at greater distances and old-fashioned marksmanship have carried the day. Also, I personally approach using any firearm with greater confidence when I know that it will shoot. With a modern revolver, the accuracy potential comes with the purchase price and is not the function of an aftermarket barrel and/or expensive gunsmithing.

When revolvers get as big as this Model 657 S&W
.41 Magnum, they are just too big for any but a
handful of shooters to hide in normal clothing.

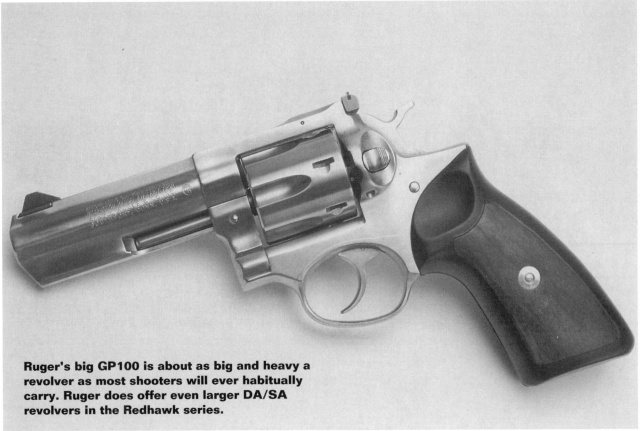

Ruger's big GP100 is about as big and heavy a
revolver as most shooters will ever habitually
carry. Ruger does offer even larger DA/SA
revolvers in the Redhawk series.

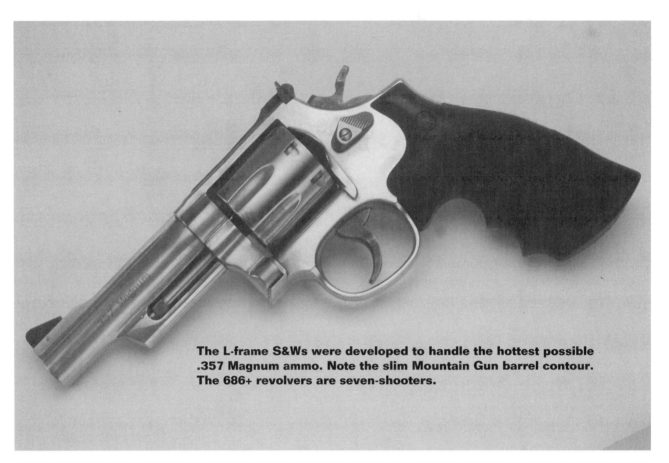

The L-frame S&Ws were developed to handle the hottest possible .357 Magnum ammo. Note the slim Mountain Gun barrel contour. The 686+ revolvers are seven-shooters.

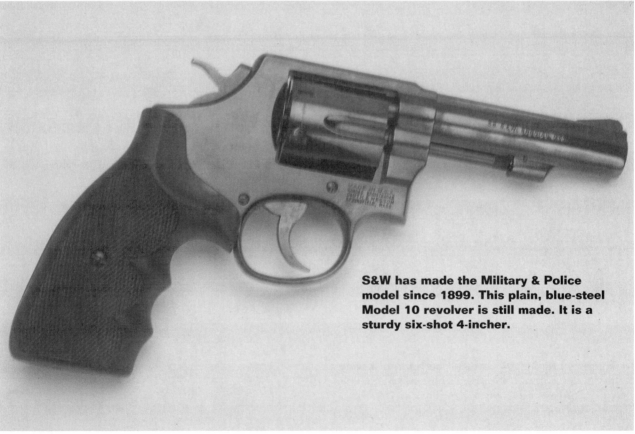

S&W has made the Military & Police model since 1899. This plain, blue-steel Model 10 revolver is still made. It is a sturdy six-shot 4-incher.

Taurus Tracker cylinders compared to show their capacities. The .41 Magnum is a five-shot, while the .357 has seven chambers.

It might be heavy to carry to the fight, but you will appreciate the recoil-absorbing heft when you fire the big Ruger.

While there is much to commend the big single-action revolvers, they are usually a bit on the large size to tuck away under street clothing.

Some N-frame S&Ws might be pressed into service as concealed-carry handguns. This one is a .45ACP Mountain Gun, a variation of the Model 625-2.

Those big DA/SA wheelguns have another option in the form of two excellent trigger modes. Further, the guns are physically shaped to facilitate using either one with considerable efficiency. The latter statement is one that might need some amplification. Many of today's efficient automatic pistols have DA or DAO triggers, but none of those guns are shaped to make shooting with the DA trigger particularly easy. That's because almost all autos have a moving slide and the shooter's hand sits well below it. The natural shape of a revolver frame allows the shooter to get a higher grip and that gives his trigger finger a better opportunity for leverage against the trigger,

leverage that allows him to sweep that trigger through a long, smooth arc. Also, because of the revolver shape, it's easy to reach up and thumb cock the hammer for a crisp, light single-action trigger pull whenever the tactical circumstances demand it. Thumb-cocking a DA/SA auto is plainly awkward.

For the purposes of classification, we will consider a large revolver to be any revolver of adequate defensive caliber fitted with a barrel of 4 inches or more. This system would have to include a number of guns with barrels 8 inches and longer. Carrying one of these long-legged brutes is difficult and presenting it from concealment can

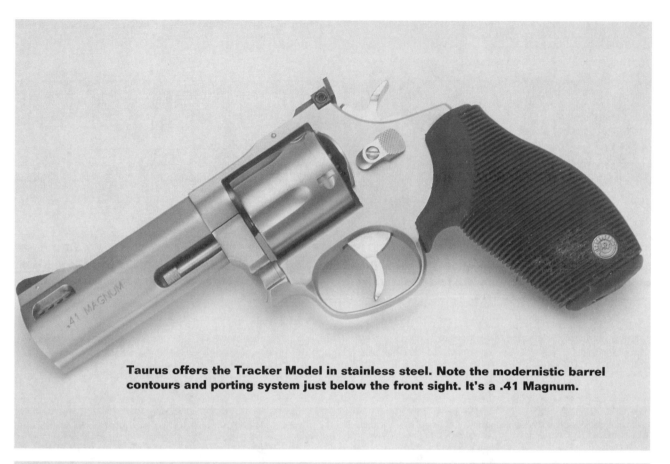

Taurus offers the Tracker Model in stainless steel. Note the modernistic barrel contours and porting system just below the front sight. It's a .41 Magnum.

You can also get a Taurus Tracker in .357 Magnum caliber. The gray finish shows it to be a light Total Titanium revolver. It's a kicker, but the rubber "Ribber" grips take the sting out of the recoil.

be a lengthy process at a time when speed is essential. For those reasons, I will not dwell on the really long barrels as we progress through a discussion of the various models in the large revolver field.

That discussion begins with the big wheelguns made by **Sturm, Ruger & Co.** While Ruger does make a huge DA/SA revolver called the Redhawk and an even larger one called the Super Redhawk, both of them are so massive as to be out of the question for concealed carry. They are sportsmen's revolvers intended for rough service as hunting handguns. Like all Rugers, they are hell for stout (I don't think Bill Ruger ever made anything flimsy in his whole life). The one revolver in the Ruger stable that is a good choice for concealed carry is the famous GP100. We took a quick look at this revolver in the chapter on medium revolvers. With a short 3-inch barrel and fixed sights, the GP100 qualifies as a medium revolver, but anything longer falls into the large category. One of the better variations of the GP100 as a defensive revolver is the stainless steel 4-incher with fixed sights and a short barrel shroud. This one is as light as they make 4-inch GPs, but it has the advantage of a relatively snag-free profile.

The most commonly encountered GP100 is the adjustable sight, long shroud 4-incher. I have one of the first of these ever produced and it continues to deliver solid performance in terms of accuracy and dependability. Ruger offers the GP100 with a long 6-inch barrel, and some sturdy individuals might find this to be a gun that could be carried under clothing. For most shooters, the best bet is going to be one of the 4-inch GP100s, preferably the fixed-sight variation. There is one model of the GP100 that is a .38 Special, but it is intended for police agencies that prohibit magnums. All other GP100 models—blue or stainless, fixed or adjustable sights, long barrel or short—are .357s. If you like your GP100—and you probably will—you can subject it to years of practice firing and not be concerned about wearing it out. This is a rugged gun.

Taurus International put a few more pages in their catalog to cover all of their large revolvers. As it is with all of the other makers, there are some Taurus wheelguns that are simply too large for concealed carry and probably too powerful for fast combat shooting. There are, however, several

other models that fit the parameters of the large concealed-carry revolver rather well and at some attractive prices. The first of those is a plain "M&P" style (to borrow the S&W designation) six-shot, fixed-sight, medium frame .38 Special 4-incher. Called the Model 82, this is basic protection in a durable gun with a lifetime warranty. There's also the Model 66, an adjustable-sight stainless or blue steel seven-shot revolver that comes with your choice of 4- or 6-inch barrels. Solid steel handguns are durable, but tend to the heavy side. A 4-inch Taurus M66 weighs 38 ounces. That is just one ounce less than a M1911A1 .45 automatic.

Top of the line for Taurus revolvers is the massive Raging Bull series. Like Ruger's Redhawks, these large revolvers are far too big and heavy to be carried by any but the most determined of handgunners. But Taurus does use the same extra-large frame for a pair of guns called the Model 44 and Model 608. These come with an optional short barrel, 4 inches in length, and they could arguably serve as concealed-carry handguns. As the model designation suggests, the 608 has *eight* .357 Magnum chambers in that big cylinder. It weighs 44 ounces. In earlier chapters, we talked about Taurus innovations in small and medium revolvers. Taurus Total Titanium revolvers have drawn a lot of favorable attention and it is this style of gun that gives Taurus a fighting chance in the large revolver concealed-carry market. They are intended for the backpacking outdoorsman, but the Taurus Trackers revolvers would also make excellent concealed-carry guns. Available in matte-finish stainless steel as well as the lightweight titanium, the Trackers are seven-shot in .357 Magnum and five-shot in .41 Magnum. The weight of a titanium Tracker is about 26 ounces.

Smith & Wesson remains the world leader in combat revolvers and has been so for all of the 20th century. Their large (barrels longer than 4 inches) revolvers come in a variety of sizes and calibers. The selection has to start with the Models 10 and 64 (blue and stainless) medium frames. This is the famous Military & Police model .38 Special revolver, which has been made in essentially the same form since 1899. The company makes the same size gun with a .357 cylinder as the model 65 in stainless steel. No one who packs either of these guns could be considered badly armed. If you have to have adjustable sights (which may be a questionable feature on a concealed-carry handgun), S&W has the Model 67 in .38 Special and the Model 66 in .357 Magnum.

In the 1970s, .357 Magnum ammunition underwent a profound change in bullet weight and bullet speed. This necessitated a change in revolver construction to produce guns with beefier barrel shanks, more resistant to high-pressure ammo. S&W's answer was the L-frame revolver—the Model 686. They are slightly larger than the K-frames, but come in a variety of different barrel lengths—2 1/2, 4, 6, and 8 3/8 inches. The 4-inch guns are good, if not ideal, choices as concealed-carry handguns. One of the better things to happen to the L-frame revolvers is the 686 Plus. This was introduced several years ago—a seven-shot cylinder. Like the other two revolver makers, S&W does make even bigger revolvers. They're called the N-frames.

A couple of those N-frames are still made with the fairly compact 4-inch barrel, but most have less practical longer barrels. From time to time, S&W makes small runs of special variations to their standard models. One of them is the so-called "Mountain Gun." This is a standard N-frame with the slim and tapered barrel of years gone by. If your choice of handguns is a large revolver, it would seem that one of the Mountain Guns is a very good choice. They have been made as .44 Magnums, .41 Magnums, .45 Long Colt, and .45 ACP. For a variety of reasons, I would consider the best of the breed to be the .45 ACP version. The whole concept has become sufficiently popular that S&W tooled up and made a slightly smaller L-frame version in .357 Magnum (seven-shot cylinder). The Mountain Guns are made in runs of a thousand or so and they are not always available. Also, we have to mention S&W's Performance Center, which cranks out short runs of all kinds of upgraded special editions.

Before we leave the subject of large revolvers, we have to consider the matter of single actions. Into this broad field goes the Colt guns (Cowboy and original Peacemaker) and all of Bill Ruger's Blackhawks, Super Blackhawks, Bisleys, and Vaqueros. There are also a number of European–made replicas of the Western handguns, and that includes some of the top-break Smith & Wessons. There are limitations to all of these guns as modern concealed-carry handguns and it is not necessarily the fact that they are far from modern. Like all of the other guns we have discussed in this chapter, the Frontier guns are large and heavy and that tends to exclude them from most people's consideration. Cartridges like the .45 S&W, .44-40, and .38-40 were originally used in handguns for the same reasons we would consider using them today. They are effective fight-stoppers.

Conclusions

CHAPTER 12

fondly recall my days as a hotshot young deputy sheriff, when I was running all over California to shoot PPC matches and just generally having a hell of a good time. At one point in that period, I became convinced that the sun would never shine on me again if I didn't have a flashy Italian sports car called a DeTomaso Pantera. Lincoln dealers were selling them then and the tab was, as I recall, about 25 grand. Now, that was a lot more than my annual stipend from the good citizens of Orange County, so the car just never materialized in my driveway. As much as I schemed and connived, I just couldn't manage to buy such an expensive set of wheels. I began to mutter the accursed "C" word and eventually I did it. I compromised on another Italian import—the Fiat 124 Sport Spyder—and we lived happily ever after. End of amusing anecdote.

But there is a point to be made here. As much as I might like to have a concealed-carry handgun the size of a Kahr but capable of carrying a 14-shot .45 magazine like a Para-Ordnance, I can't have it. Such a pistol does not and cannot exist. Therefore, I have to compromise on something that falls somewhere in-between. It's either carry the Kahr with a lower capacity of less powerful cartridges, pack the Para-Ordnance with a very large weight and bulk, or compromise on something in-between. Just as I once found a lower-priced sports car to be an acceptable compromise, so can you find a handgun that fits your needs. In a sense, that is what this book is all about. Understand at the outset that if you are happy with the big gun and can manage to habitually carry it, so much the better. At the other pole, if you settle on a very small handgun and always tuck that one away on your person, you are well armed.

We have covered a great variety of different handguns in chapters 6 through 11 of this book. And in earlier chapters, we went into considerable detail to describe what makes an adequate personal

Most shooters will eventually compromise on something between the big Para-Ordnance .45 and the Kahr Mk9 in 9mm Luger.

Technological advances keep pace with the demand for lighter and lighter handguns. S&W is not the only maker to offer light revolvers in powerful calibers.

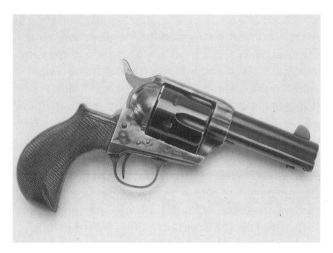

Make your selection with care. This Cimarron Thunderer in .45 Colt is fine handgun, but requires an inordinate amount of time to master.

If you choose to go with a cocked-and-locked carry and have scant experience with the system, accept the need for first-class training at Gunsite or Thunder Ranch.

defense handgun. By the standards thus established, anything you read about in this volume is an adequate gun. Remember that adequate guns don't stop lethal confrontations, but bullets delivered from adequate guns by shooters with adequate skills do. It is up to you to spend the time to develop your skills with your chosen firearm. The best way to do that is to go to one of the good defensive shooting schools around the country.

By virtue of personal experience with Gunsite Academy and Thunder Ranch, I can endorse both of them enthusiastically. I am aware of a number of other schools that enjoy excellent reputations. The beauty of a good beginning school, even for a man or woman already familiar with guns and shooting, is that it gets you on the right track and provides a blueprint for continued practice at home. With the basic course behind you, you can maintain your skills with diligent practice at home, then go back to your school for continuing education at more advanced levels. Both of the major schools—Thunder Ranch and Gunsite Academy—have several levels of advanced training that teach more involved shooting and tactical skills. Most students find shooting in

You must understand the complexities of your pistol's operation. (A)The TDA S&W auto's safety/decocker is off and a DA pull will fire the gun. (B) The safety/decocker is off and the hammer is cocked, so SA pressure on the trigger will fire the gun. (C) Turning the safety/decocker down lowers the hammer, but trigger pressure won't fire the gun. For speedy use, don't leave the gun in this condition.

The Kahr pistols come in several sizes. All are superb pocket autos.

The Sig P239 and Kahr Micro are the author's top choices in really small automatic pistols.

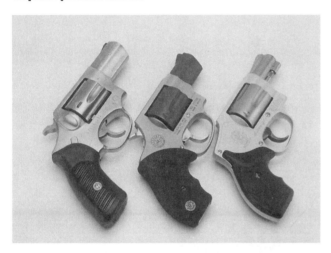

Any one of these small revolvers will fill the bill. Any hammer gun probably needs to have the spur removed for optimum use from under clothing.

The mid-sized Glocks (G19, G23, G32) or the Steyr M and S models are best bets in the medium auto field.

these simulated gunfight scenarios to be interesting and challenging.

Before we get into discussing the selection process, determining what's right for you, let's look at a few principles. First of all, I believe that you should choose a gun that is as big and powerful as you can regularly carry on your person and effectively manage in close-range, high-stress shooting exercises. For a great many shooters (maybe even the *majority* of shooters), that really is not a whole lot of gun. Size and weight become big considerations when you are contemplating an object that will literally become a part of your lifestyle. And it also follows that a gun that is small enough for you to habitually carry, but

powerful enough to decisively resolve an unwanted fight, is probably going to have enough muzzle blast and recoil to be difficult to manage.

If there is any way you can shoot an assortment of handguns before you settle on one, you would be well advised to do so. What seems to be the neatest little gun in the world when you are standing at the counter of the gun store just might turn out to be an uncontrollable beast when you get it to the range. Also, consult as many authorities and references as you can before you buy. Be cautious about the advice of gun store commandos. I have witnessed teenage clerks (who have been reading gun magazines for a few months) dispensing life and death wisdom as

The G36 is one of the author's pets in the medium auto field. It is a single-column, 6+1 .45 ACP pistol.

You would be in good shape with a Performance Center Short 40 in your pocket, fanny pack, or concealment holster.

Medium revolver? How about a Taurus Total Titanium 2-inch in .44 Special? It is light enough to carry and powerful enough to stop fights.

Big autos? It's either of two classics—the 8+1 Government Model .45 (Springfield version shown) or the 13+1 9mm Browning Hi-Power.

Either of these S&Ws is a top choice in a medium revolver. The 296 Centennial is a .44 Special and the 386PD is a .357. Both are lightweights.

The author has fired thousands of rounds from this P226 .357 Sig, a model and caliber he favors greatly in large autos.

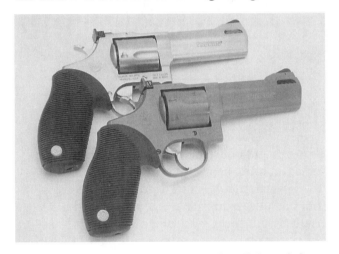

Either of the Taurus Trackers, either lightweight or all stainless, would be highly satisfactory defensive guns in the large revolver category.

If pressed to choose just one large revolver for concealed carry, this would probably be the author's gun—a 686+ Mountain Gun in .357 Magnum.

though they were selling TVs or toasters. And remember you are shopping for a *concealed-carry* handgun and not a *home-defense* handgun.

If a particular handgun is adequate for concealed carry, it is also adequate—but not necessarily ideal—for home defense. Much of this book is all wrapped up resolving the mass versus performance dichotomy to help you choose something that you will have in your pocket or purse when away from home. Carryable size and weight are very important. But if the handgun you are choosing is not to be carried outside your place of residence, why worry about how concealable it is? In your home or apartment, you can easily and

safely store a relatively large and powerful handgun that is easier to manage than a featherweight when the need arises. Don't confuse the two classes of handguns.

Most Americans don't experience life-and-death struggle as part of their daily lives. That extends to most policemen, who obviously do have a far greater chance of violent conflict. But if a violent attack does come your way, it is most likely to be sudden and without warning. It may even be in a completely unexpected locale. There have been instances of attacks on citizens in such unlikely places as public restrooms, parking garages, and elevators. You used to be pretty safe

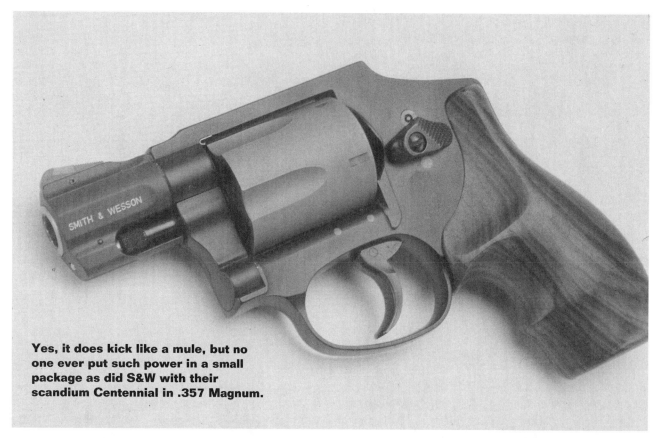

Yes, it does kick like a mule, but no one ever put such power in a small package as did S&W with their scandium Centennial in .357 Magnum.

when you were in your car, but carjacking is now a fact of life in major cities. Wide-open country was also once pretty secure, but there have been instances of criminal roadblocks on isolated roads, and even personal assaults on the foot trails of national parks and forests. Under these conditions, a good handgun can be a workable tool for crisis resolution, but simple awareness of one's circumstances and surroundings may keep you out of a fight in the first place. If you can avoid conflict, do so. Shooting a criminal attacker, no matter what the justification, is going to be a messy business. Common sense and compiled statistics tell us that an attack is most likely to happen at very close range and with no warning. For that reason, I believe that you should be capable of getting your handgun into action with extreme speed. I also believe the gun should be capable of firing instantly.

And this feature brings us back to the comparison of various kinds of guns. More to the point, what features of a defensive handgun are most valuable and why? Consider the fact that for almost all of the 20th century, the DA/SA revolver was the almost universal choice of defensive

shooters and policemen who had to carry a handgun for instant use. When the first of the double-action triggers were added to revolvers that had always had single-action ones, the resulting guns were welcomed heartily. Why? Simple—you could shoot them quicker. A DA/SA or DAO revolver is still a viable choice, despite lower capacity and greater bulk. All you need do to make a wheelgun go is sweep that trigger through a long arc. It's the same for every shot and you can learn to work a DA revolver with a fairly short training cycle.

When the autos came along, we embraced them enthusiastically. Most of the reason was that quick-to-load magazine in the butt and the fact that the gun reloaded its own chamber. But we have been uneasy for a century about the fact the automatic pistol cocks itself after firing a shot, so that another short pressure on the trigger causes it to fire another shot. At first, the armies of the world carried the automatic gun with the chamber empty and the hammer down. That somehow seemed safer. The safety was deemed to be a very important control and we paid a lot of attention to it. Then someone noticed that with a little effort,

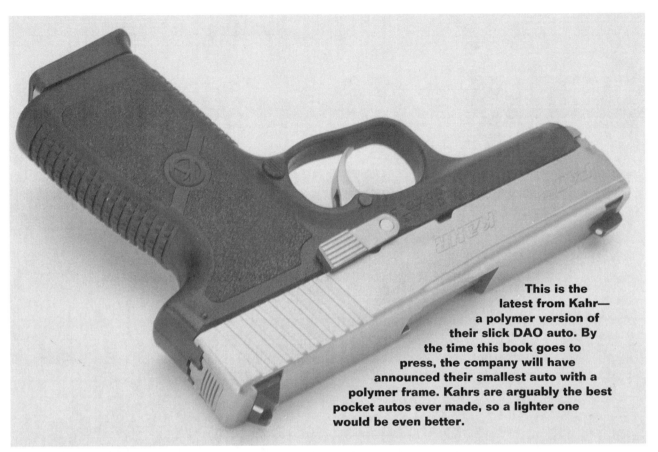

This is the latest from Kahr— a polymer version of their slick DAO auto. By the time this book goes to press, the company will have announced their smallest auto with a polymer frame. Kahrs are arguably the best pocket autos ever made, so a lighter one would be even better.

This is one of two pistols the author most commonly carries—a steel Commander .45 Auto, customized by Wayne Novak. You can't do much better than this.

Technology has raised the power ceiling in light revolvers to the point where we can now have a .357 Magnum revolver weighing less than 15 ounces, fully loaded.

you could add a double-action trigger to an automatic pistol that had always worked on the basis of a single-action one.

Since the introduction of the DA/SA auto in 1929, we have struggled to make our pistols behave like revolvers.

The DA/SA pistol is a common instrument and the best of them are pretty fine handguns. But I have to wonder why we can't accept the fact that the short, crisp 4- to 5-pound trigger of a single-action auto is the best and quickest way to get a handgun shooting when you need to do so. And that is despite the fact that you must carry it cocked and locked, depressing the safety before firing. Not only is a single-action trigger best for the first shot, it's better for quick and accurate delivery of second and subsequent shots. If the safety is properly positioned, the shooter easily learns to pop it off as a part of the draw stroke. Training is the key to getting the most out of any handgun, but training is absolutely essential to working the single-action auto.

In the last 20 years, we have seen a remarkable explosion of systems to make autos carry more safely and shoot more rapidly. The milestone system was that of Gaston Glock and his unique Safe Action series of pistols. For import criteria, BATF classifies the Glock as a DAO, but that is only partially true. If Glocks were not so good, why are they so widely copied? Even their major competitors have found one way or another to evade Glock's patents and produce a pistol that has some kind of DAO trigger system that feels like it was a single action. Suffice it to say that a great deal of ingenuity has gone into building better automatic pistols (including some very small ones) and you can find guns that are suited to your own needs. With this kind of variety, it's easy to make a mistake, so do your homework before you buy.

At this point in the book, and at the urging of the publishers, I am going to get into some specific recommendations. I have personal prejudices and preferences just like anyone else, but I hope I will not come off as sounding preachy or pontifical. I speak initially from the basis of many years of interest in firearms and from a number of years in the United States Marines and as a deputy sheriff. I have been a competitive shooter in several different disciplines. For the past 20 years I have been writing for one or more of the major gun magazines and for the last 15 of those years, that has been my full-time employment. With some exceptions, I have been primarily concerned with handguns. In the course of that time, I have had virtually every one of the major handguns for shooting evaluation. I believe this has put me in a unique position to judge what is good and what isn't. Just a few years ago, I began to make periodic trips to the major shooting schools to write stories on them. In doing so, I have used a variety of different guns to make comparative judgements about them. Believe me, a week at Gunsite or Thunder Ranch is a good test of a handgun. Throughout all of this experience, I have made a strong effort to be objective. And I carry a gun with me every day of my life.

So let's get on with the program. Consider the small auto first, since it is the newest gun style on the handgun scene. It is pretty tough to shrink an automatic pistol that's a 9mm Luger or larger down to carrying size, but there are a few excellent ones out there. As fond as I am of the M1911 format autos, I should be more enthused about the Colt, Kimber, and Springfield little .45s. My experience with them suggests that they are a trifle too temperamental. With the attention of a good pistolsmith, they might be pretty decent guns. There are also three small Glocks that seem to work beautifully and are about as small as you can make a Glock—the G26, G27, and G33. While they have great reliability, these little Glocks are a bit bulky and hard to hide.

I have two top choices in the little auto category. Look at the Sig P239, a single-column DA/SA pistol in 9mm, .40 S&W, and .357 Sig calibers. The plain decocker system is simple and easy to use, the trigger pull is decent, and the gun is accurate and reliable right out of the box. It's also small enough to hide quite easily. So is my top choice for a small auto—any of the Kahr autos. Any Kahr—the larger K9 and K40 or the micro-sized Mk9 or Mk40—is small enough to hide easily. Their newest is a light polymer version of the K9 and it effectively resolves the only complaint anyone ever made about the Kahr—weight. I hope the company will produce a polymer Micro and maybe even a little .45. Kahrs are beautifully made pistols you can trust.

Small revolvers are still viable choices in

defensive handguns, although they suffer from a cartridge capacity that's a little less than we might like it. Most commonly, that capacity is five rounds. If you can handle a little more weight, try one of Bill Ruger's SP101 revolvers in .357 Magnum. This is a rather heavy little gun, but it is built like a battleship and will last for most shooters' lifetimes. Ruger makes one variety of the SP101 with a bobbed hammer. This is the gun you want. About the only way Ruger could improve the SP101 would be to build it with some form of lightweight frame. Another excellent choice is one of the little Taurus Model 85s, with either the titanium or aluminum frame. Taurus makes the 85 with a steel frame, but the same gun that's much lighter is a better choice. If appearance is part of your selection criteria, Taurus makes their titanium 85s in a choice of colors, several of which are strikingly handsome.

Smith & Wesson makes more small revolvers than any of the other makers. Most of them are built on the J-frame. If weight is less important to you than most shooters, S&W makes three guns in stainless steel—the Chiefs Special, Bodyguard, and Centennial. All are good choices and the Centennial, which is a DAO with an enclosed internal hammer, is one of the best concealed-carry handguns of all time. Just as this book was finishing up, S&W introduced the scandium frame series of revolvers. They have titanium cylinders and weigh in right at 12 ounces. Scandium, alloyed with aluminum, makes for a frame that is sufficiently shock-resistant to take the pounding of .357 Magnum ammo. The S&W model 340Sc is a nasty kicker, but it is still the lightest really powerful handgun we have yet seen.

We spent a lot of time looking at many different medium autos in Chapter 8, so narrowing the field is tough. Although certain aspects of the gun are controversial, I personally like the Steyr M and Steyr S quite a lot. I question the need for a safety on a DAO, but they located the safety on this one well out of the way. Steyrs follow the modern trend—DAO, polymer frame, 10+1 capacity. Naturally, three different Glocks are high on my list. They are the G19, G23, and G32 in 9mm, .40 S&W, and .357 Sig.

If you can spend a little more money, the S&W Performance Center Shorty 40 is a great gun with TDA lockwork.

But another Glock is a personal favorite. It is the G36, Glock's first gun with a single-column magazine. Other Glocks have always felt bulky in my hand, but the G36 is flatter and plainly feels better to me. Best of all, this is Glock's long-awaited medium .45 ACP pistol. My pet medium autos are two Sigs. One is the P245, a single column .45 ACP pistol of concealable proportions and weight. The other is the 10+1 P229 in .40 S&W and .357 Sig. These are 10+1 pistols about the same size as the P245, but just slightly thicker. I liked Sigs the minute I picked up the first one, mostly because of the trigger system. It is a DA/SA and has a decocker. I have read pages of criticism of a DA/SA trigger system, most of it centered on the fact that the shooter's hand needs a different "set" for the first and second shots. For me, that simply isn't true when I am shooting one of my Sigs.

The three different revolver makers make medium revolvers. All of them have something in the 3-inch and/or medium-frame bracket. Ruger's gun is the fixed sight GP100 with 3-inch barrel. Like all Rugers, it's a rugged gun. There are several Taurus revolvers that fall into this bracket, but I like the Total Titanium compact frame 2-incher in .44 Special. The gun also comes in .357 Magnum, .41 Magnum, and .45 Colt, but the .44 Special has a better range of good, big-bullet defensive loads made for it. There are even a number of Cowboy Action Shooting loads that would serve beautifully.

Smith & Wesson makes several great defensive medium revolvers, including an unusual humpbacked Centennial .44 Special on a lightweight aluminum L-frame. My favorite in this class is a seven-shot .357 Magnum on a light scandium frame. As this is written, the company plans to offer this gun in a dull black finish and with sensible fixed sights. I have had advanced samples of the scandium series of guns and I found them to be vicious kickers. But they are not recreational plinkers for Saturday morning fun, they are crisis guns intended to save your life. I doubt if you will ever feel the recoil if you had to use one for its intended purpose.

Dozens of large automatic pistols are available, but one dominates the scene. It is the Government Model pistol, the venerable Colt M1911A1. It's big and weighs 39 ounces, but there is no better automatic pistol to have in your hand when the trouble starts. The .45 is currently made

Considering all of the handguns evaluated for this book, the author ranks the S&W Model 340 PD AirLite as the best all-around concealed carry handgun of them all.

by Colt, Kimber, and Springfield, as well as a host of other makers. It is unfortunately true that an entry-level Government Model pistol made by any maker will require the attention of a good pistolsmith before you take put it in service. It is also true that a shooter needs serious training before he can get the most from the gun. The M1911A1 may be the king, but many shooters like the Commander version of the same gun. With an aluminum frame and a slightly shorter barrel and slide, the Commander still delivers .45 ACP clout and carries much easier. Remember compromise? The Commander is one of the better ones you may ever make.

There are other large autos and one of the best is the venerable Browning Hi-Power. It has the same cocked-and-locked style as the Colt and may be the most reliable pistol made, right out of the carton. I also like the big Sig .45 called the P220. It has the same lockwork as the smaller Sigs and I am comfortable with it. Another possibility in a large auto is the unusual Walther P99 or S&W SW99. An unusual but reliable pistol with three distinctively different trigger modes, the 99 is a good choice.

We also have to take a brief look at upgraded M1911A1 pistols made by Wilson, Baer, Brown, and both the Kimber and Springfield Custom Shops. The Government Model pistol has become so popular in the last decade that those who make them are no longer taking stock pistols and modifying them. Instead, they are building guns from scratch with the beavertails, extended safeties, premium barrels, checkering, and other features customers want. It has become a highly competitive business, which has the beneficial effect of driving the prices down. The best buys in these "everything you need, nothing you don't" pistols come from the home of pistol training—Gunsite Academy's Custom Shop in Paulden, Arizona.

Not many big revolvers are used as concealed-carry handguns, but some hardy shooters do manage to pack them. Ruger's big GP100, with or without adjustable sights, is a great choice. So is the much lighter Total Titanium Taurus Tracker series. You can get the 4-inch Tracker in either steel or titanium, but the titanium is lighter by a good margin. Seven shots in .357 and five in .41

magnum, these are excellent choices. My personal preference would have to be the S&W Mountain revolver on the L-frame. I have always liked the looks of that slim and stylish barrel and you can't argue with the oh-so-smooth DA trigger action of the Smith & Wesson revolver.

That takes us through a series of my top choices in concealed-carry handguns. I freely concede that there are a great many other guns that might serve you as well as the ones I have mentioned have served me. Elsewhere in the book, I mentioned that I would describe the guns that I actually do use. There are several guns that I carry at one time or another and I don't see any reason why most readers could not do the same. Basically, it comes down to a pair of handgun types.

When the weather is such that I am wearing a coat or vest, my preferred handgun is a Colt Commander in .45 ACP. The gun has been extensively customized by Wayne Novak and has a Bar-Sto barrel installed. I also use a Lightweight Commander, which was built up by Ted Yost at Gunsite. The two pistols are really the same guns, differing only in the weight of the receiver. The Novak gun is steel, while the Yost pistol is aluminum. Both are utterly reliable and I have trained with them to the point that I am reasonably skillful in using them. But both are fairly heavy and bulky pistols, so I have settled on another gun that is lighter and more carryable under any conditions of dress or circumstances. This handgun is the one that I believe is the very best all-around choice for any handgunner at any time.

The gun is a Smith & Wesson Model 340 PD Centennial. It has the scandium frame and weighs 12 ounces. It is, of course, a .357 Magnum and I am carrying it with a heavy-bullet Magnum load. I am fully aware that it kicks like hell, but if I fire the gun under circumstances of genuine need, I doubt if I will remember the kick. The major reason for making such a gun my top choice is the simple fact that it is the best of several small and light handguns that I can carry habitually without discomfort. Centennials have a distinctive shape that conceals easily and comes out of an Uncle Mike's pocket holster slick as grease. And this is the gun that I recommend to readers as the best all around concealed-carry handgun of them all.

About the Author

For nearly two decades, Wiley Clapp has been writing about firearms in general and handguns in particular. His stories have appeared in most major gun magazines—*Guns & Ammo, Shooting Times, HandGunning, Gun World, Combat Handguns* and others—and he is the author or coauthor of four books. Clapp is currently a field editor for *The American Rifleman* and handgun editor for *Guns & Ammo*.

Clapp was an infantry officer with the United States Marine Corps, with service in the early years of the Vietnam War. He is retired from the Orange County Sheriff's Department in California. Formerly an active competitor in several handgun disciplines, he is well known in the firearms industry. Working from a great deal of police and military experience, as well as an extensive firearms library, Clapp continues to produce several dozen magazine articles every year.

For this book, he obtained samples of virtually every handgun mentioned, evaluating each for its suitability as a concealed-carry handgun for 21st-century Americans. The result is a unique selection guide for those who have made the decision—as has the author—to go habitually armed.